JUMPING:
Learning and Teaching

Col. Gudin de Vallerin on Princesse des Ternes.

JUMPING:
Learning and Teaching

by
Jean Froissard,
Ecuyer-Professeur, F.F.S.E.

translated by Lily Powell-Froissard

PELHAM BOOKS

First published in Great Britain by
PELHAM BOOKS LIMITED
52 *Bedford Square*
*London, W.C.*1
1972

7207 0489 8

*Printed lithographically in Great Britain by
Hollen Street Press Ltd at Slough and
bound by James Burn at Esher, Surrey*

This work is dedicated to **Colonel Gudin de Vallerin,** a great performer and teacher, whose book has convinced me of the value of written instruction.

Contents

Foreword

by
DORIAN WILLIAMS

The increase in interest in show jumping in countries all over the world during the last twenty years has been quite remarkable: In some countries phenomenal.

This has not been limited, as some people think, to those who watch on television, though certainly in many countries, particularly perhaps in Britain where the big shows can command audiences of upwards of 10 million viewers at a single transmission. Equally a new interest has been aroused amongst riders.

The standard of show jumping as a result has never been higher—at the top. A high degree of professionalism, not to say perfectionism, has now become commonplace amongst those riders whose names have become household words: Steinkraus, Chapot, Winkler, Schockemöhle, d'Inzeo, Pessoa, d'Oriola, Mancinelli, Broome, Robeson, Harvey Smith and lady riders such as Kathy Kusner, Marion Coakes, Alison Westwood, Janou Lefèbvre, Guilia Serventi, Carol Hoffman, Anneli Drummond Hay.

But for every star there are a hundred, perhaps a thousand ordinary riders with ambitions and aspirations of varying degrees.

It is for this legion of enthusiasts that this book of Jean Froissard will be so helpful.

It is, to say the least, extraordinarily comprehensive. It emphasises—rightly without apology—the importance of basic training, training on the ground, as well as the more easily acceptable training of horse and rider over fences.

In many ways one of the most rewarding developments in the

last few years is the acceptance by those at the top of the importance of proper basic schooling. It is virtually true to say that no
rider will get to the top without it.

Unfortunately, so many who have all the enthusiasm and in
many ways the ability to reach the top just do not understand
what is meant by basic training. They will find this book enormously
helpful. In one volume they have got it all.

Unusual in a book of the type, Jean Froissard brings what one
might almost call an intellectual approach to the whole subject.
This, without doubt, makes it different from the ordinary run of
the mill book and it suggests, justifiably, that the author has in
addition to his practical knowledge and experience given the whole
subject deep, logical thought. Readers of this book will agree that
it was worth while.

Acknowledgments

For many of the photographs and some important information for this book I am indebted to the National Federations of Spain and Italy, the American Olympic Committee, L'Année Hippique, L'Information Hippique, Mr. Leslie Lane, the brothers d' Inzeo, Col. de Saint-André, Ecuyer-en-chef of the Cadre Noir, and for several of the line drawings in the bit section to Captain Hartley Edwards of "Riding."

Needless to say that I have once more had the faithful collaboration of Lily, my wife and translator, and of David, my son and guinea pig.

JUMPING:
Learning and Teaching

Part I

The Education of the Rider

(Photo Josserand)

CHAPTER ONE

Of Equestrian Unity

S how jumping, big time or small, is a specialization for both horse and rider; but "specializing"—that is, studying in depth part of a field of knowledge—is desultory, unless it represents the ultimate choice of a knowledgeable all-around practitioner. Yet young riders hasten to mount their "hobby horses," with a grand indifference toward the other two thirds of equitation, and the time-honored twin concepts of the "good all-around horseman," the "good all-around horse" have almost acquired the ring of nostalgia. Today's riders, not only the very young, enter the arena with nary a qualm, on the sole premise that their horses have the power to clear the pole at a certain height and that their instructors have given them the "simplified course in instant horsemanship," which consists of chanting, "steady, steady," five times during the last ten strides before the jump. This incantation is no open sesame.

It may be argued that John Champion was a sorry pupil in the school and has blithely ignored classic teachings ever since, and that Queen of the Course burst onto the show scene after the sketchiest of preparations. Such very rare exceptions still confirm the rule and leave it open to speculation how much better both horse and rider might have done with the added advantage of classical training. Their intrinsic qualities count, of course, but optimal success will only come if such talent is developed through the progressive, rational training only classical equitation can give.

This training establishes a succession of goals. For the horse: impulsion, without which nothing is possible; suppling; finally balance. For the rider: seat, steadiness (*fixity*), pliancy (*correspondence*), and independence of the aids; later a feel for pace, balance, distance, that is, the acquisition and refinement of equestrian tact. Primarily, it never loses sight of the fact that ALL EQUITATION IS AS ONE, resting in all its branches on three mainstays, *Impulsion*, *Engagement* and *Balance*.

Depending on origins and aptitudes, all three are present, to varying degrees, in the never ridden horse who can modify them at will but whose troubles begin when he is to do so at the rider's prompting. They are physical and moral difficulties, the latter requiring priority; for winning the horse's confidence is three quarters of the road to his submission. Therefore, not to push the horse to rebellion through excessive fatigue or prolonged subjection, the trainer must know how to limit his demands. Only then—after a minimum of (never overestimated) submission has been obtained— may he begin to supple the body by exercises enabling the horse to modify, as prompted, without effort or resistance, his impulsion, engagement and balance.

What is the meaning of these three, the most important terms in equitation?

Impulsion is a moral attribute expressed through the horse's permanent urge energetically to move forward, increased, stored or channeled by the rider's rational application of his aids. It is the very soul of equitation and should not be confused with that most physical of properties, speed, which is but the horse's rate of travel.

Engagement of the hind legs is a consequence of haunches lowered through the bending of hocks, stifle and coxo-femural joints, causing a more advanced position of hind legs under the mass. With the right intensity and accuracy of this engagement, the joints and muscles of the quarters act like coiled springs, able to give the horse the maximum release needed for a given jump or movement.

Balance lies in the rational distribution, between forehand and quarters, of the horse's own body weight and that of the rider. The better this balance, the more mobile the center of gravity, endowing the horse with easier, more fluent gaits, on the flat and over fences, an unlabored mobility only achieved through training.*

What are the parts played by these factors, then, in the Olympic

* For other definitions, see *Glossary of Technical Terms*.

disciplines, Dressage, Stadium Jumping and Cross Country? Let us each time, and far from arbitrarily, begin with cross-country riding, it being of the three activities the most congenial with the horse's nature.

IMPULSION definitely is the *Cross Country* horse's foremost quality, the permanent urge to advance and the energy to do so, allowing him to take natural obstacles within his physical capacities and capabilities for their rational use. Though speed—less important in Stadium Jumping and even less so in Dressage—is very helpful, impulsion still takes precedence; for what effectiveness has speed unless touched off by impulsion?

In *Stadium Jumping*, and incidentally even more so in Dressage, the rider's principal preoccupation is the increase of flagging impulsion. While at Cross Country the horse uses his speed in order to overcome difficulties and spare himself excessive muscle strain, in the arena he must summon all his muscular resources. If even here he may utilize his speed to some extent, he does so only to be checked after each jump and consequently have to duplicate the effort at the next, without relaxing morally or physically.

In *Dressage* where, despite slow gaits, each movement requires considerable energy, without any stimulant, such as the excitement of a fence to take, artistically valid work is quite impossible without maximum impulsion at the base.

In sum, impulsion is a moral attribute, the permanent urge to advance, not sluggishly but energetically, in response to the rider's every challenge with all he has got physically; it is the horse's cardinal virtue, never to be neglected. While necessary in all forms of equitation, its importance increases as does the distance separating the horse from his natural environment and the problems to solve become ever more alien and less comprehensible. Undoubtedly, he will more easily understand a series of essentially similar obstacles to be taken in the open country at a normal pace, along more or less straight lines, than a cramped and tortuously designed course in an indoor ring which, between obstacle and obstacle, forces him incessantly to modify his speed and balance and practically to take standing jumps. Even greater impulsion is, of course, required when, restricted to a rectangle, he is to give all he has got, morally and physically, without, under his eyes, a tangible difficulty to overcome.

ENGAGEMENT, on the other hand, is a physical quality on whose intensity and accuracy depends the forward movement and to some extent the balance. Yet the value of engagement depends on impulsion, the moral attribute, the urge to advance. In fact, usable for good or evil, engagement may be equally pronounced in the refusing horse and in the one about to jump.

Cantering on the flat, the engagement allows for a totally forward-oriented release; in jumping, this release, though forward, strains primarily upward; in dressage, while present in the different movements, it is more supple, more fluent, more controlled, as different as the ballet dancer's leap from the athlete's. Thus it follows that engagement cannot always be the same, must correspond to the movement or jump intended, the more so since the balance factor also enters into it and is partly modified, as we shall see, by the form of the engagement.

In *Cross Country*, guided by his instinct of self-preservation, the horse takes upon himself, totally or almost so, the problems of balance and engagement. The rider but attends to their stability or, if need be, to their reestablishment, but does not have to prompt them constantly (natural balance and engagement).

In *Stadium Jumping* things are different. Since the horse has little or no occasion to use speed for jumping, he must make maximum use of his capacity for release; i.e., of the engagement of his hind legs.

This problem is aggravated by the balance problem which, as will be seen, is closely tied in with the very vital engagement question; and all of it is further complicated by such man-made difficulties as intricate obstacle combinations and tricky distances on the course which the horse is unable to solve by himself. It is up to the rider to solve these totally or partially alone, on the basis of the faculties and training of his mount, and here the horse must trust him absolutely and unshakably, having to defer to human decision which, even when right, frequently runs counter to his instinct.

In *Dressage* the rider is totally in charge of the engagement. The releases he must prompt are of a much greater variety and thus more finely shaded. The touchstone of this kind of engagement is no longer intensity, but the particular accuracy which best serves the intended movement.

BALANCE is something the horse is able, at his own or at his rider's initiative, to modify in three different ways: elevating the base of the neck and approaching head to body; a more pronounced engagement of his hind legs; or a combination of both.

Natural balance varies in quality with conformation, particularly of the neck, its orientation and that of the head, and with the horse's skill in using them. Once more we meet with the importance of engagement which is instrumental not only in release but in the modification of balance. It is needless to prove the importance of balance, no one disputes it, no more in cross-country riding than in stadium jumping or dressage; but let us look into its meaning as applied to each of the three disciplines.

At *Cross Country*, where speed is more or less constant at a fluent gait, the horse will settle into a given balance and rarely shift it. Since the pace is pretty fast, the base is rather broad, balance therefore very stable. The rider only intervenes at critical moments.

In *Stadium Jumping*, knowing the difficulties ahead of which the horse is unaware, he is as much in charge of balance as of engagement. Obviously, the extent of his contribution depends on the difficulties of the course, his knowledge and his tact, as much as on his horse's faculties. The more knowledgeable the rider and the better schooled his horse, the more of the initiative falls to the man. One way or another, the horse must, in this branch of equitation, be able to quickly shift his balance, whether at his own initiative or the rider's, and do so from the first fence to the last.

In *Dressage* the horse's instinct must subside completely, leaving the initiative to the rider who establishes the convenient balance. Since this kind of work requires collected gaits (elevation of the base of the neck plus flexion from the poll, combined with engagement), the base is shortened and the balance far less stable than across country. The swifter and tighter the succession of required movements, the more necessary becomes near-perfect balance for the horse to operate the transition with ease and the rider to make imperceptible use of his aids.

This review of the three mainstays of equitation and their application to the three disciplines has incidentally shown to which, if varying, degrees man and horse must be able to communicate, ranging from an occasional give and take to perfect and instantaneous obedience. Only rational exercise will make this kind of athlete of a horse, with wind, muscle and suppleness physically to obey his rider and to make maximum use of his "springs," thereby acquiring that coveted air of grace and lightness; yet none of these physical assets can be attained without the prerequisite of a submission valid and fruitful only because generous and offered "joyously." It is perhaps in this omnipresent prerequisite for the conquest of the horse—even more than in the ubiquity of impulsion, engagement and balance—that we find conclusive proof of the equestrian unity.

CHAPTER TWO

The Position

The position is a means, not an end. The very best can supplement but not replace the two essentials, feeling and being with one's horse. Yet it is of great help in learning both. At a halt it is easily defined; but as soon as the horse begins to move, the horseman wanting to remain with it must do so too. Since position is by definition static and horsemanship dynamic, the long established term must be understood as a succession of constant shifts by which we go along with our mount. These shifts enable us not only to stay *on* him, of course, but to feel, and stay *with* him; to use our aids so easily, efficiently and rationally that we hardly encumber him and are comfortable ourselves.

The Position of the Rider in the School

In *manège* we sit squarely on our buttocks, pushed forward to the utmost, weighing evenly on the saddle; thighs turned effortlessly on their flats, dropping by the simple weight of legs which stretch naturally; the backs of the knees pliant; the calves in pressureless contact with the horse; heels lowered naturally and toes turned up when with, dropping freely when without, stirrups. Loins and hips supple; the upper body relaxed and straight; shoulders back and level; arms half-bent, elbows close to the body, both without constraint; wrists held up, though lower than the elbows, forming an extension of the forearms; thumbs up; head straight, relaxed, well out of the shoulders. Since such a position does not require muscular contraction, it can be held indefinitely and without fatigue.

The essence of this definition emphasizes suppleness, the absence of constraint. What minor variations may have occurred en route from the eighteenth century and de La Guérinière to the contemporary Cavalry School of Saumur are of language rather than ideas, and geographically speaking, the German horseman Wätjen gives a like definition in *Dressage Riding*, with equal emphasis on suppleness.

Let purists argue endlessly over the meaning of each word, the exact place for each part of leg or thigh; what we want is a general position as close as possible to efficiency, logic and nature. Hairsplitting has always been part of the sport and always will be. French riders, for example, are still engaged in a little "cold war of positions," dating back to the thirties when Danloux, then Equerry-in-Chief at Saumur, tried to have a new "official" jumping position adopted, which could not help but influence the general position. Arguments began to fly, principally on paper, and the more each side tried to clarify their stand, the more they managed to obscure it, the most militant on each ironically, if not unusually, emulators rather than originators.

How do you reconcile such apparent, if verbal, scission with the fact that whenever I rode where position scored important points and before juries composed of both factions, some of my individual movements were sometimes criticized but my position, most emphatically and *unanimously*, never? Since under the circumstances I should automatically have dissatisfied one faction or the other, it would seem that there is more to position than meets the eye.

There is. You cannot ride all horses in exactly the same manner, less so when mutual acquaintance is of recent date. There are, of course, unforgivable deviations which counteract balance and the use of the aids, such as tightly pressed on knees, legs shooting out forward, heels up with toes out, all bad faults in the school; but who cares if the flat of the thigh is in total contact with the saddle, so long as the legs themselves are well placed? Nobody will come and take a peek. People will forever argue over the respective advantages and disadvantages of pressing on thighs or knees or calves in an emergency; yet truly, they are arguments which stand or fall with their exponents. Tall riders tend to close their legs, shorter ones their knees, and I find the results ostensibly the same. While a faulty jumping position entailing faulty balance is serious, wanting to pay attention to a slip of the stirrup or a tip of the toe is pure childishness. Our own concern here is the typical position of the rider on the course, which is designed to let him accompany and not cramp his horse while using his aids normally, a position easily modified, if need be, at short notice. The most important factor at the moment of the jump, indubitably, is balance; i.e., the combined balance of horse and rider. If the rider happens to break it through a fault of his own, the horse will commit a fault or at least find his task that much more difficult, hardly a boon for morale-building.

The Position of the Rider on the Course

Rather than seated in the saddle, the rider is now suspended over it, leaning on his stirrups, the upper body slightly forward, the loins supply held up, the head well out of the shoulders, eyes

The rider's position on the course. (Photo Michel Alexis)

on the fence to come. The shoulders as relaxed as the elbows which are held, half-bent, slightly away from the body, the wrists, extending straight from the forearms, are forward of the withers. The thighs and legs should have maximum adherence to saddle and horse, without inhibiting the free play of hip, knee and ankle joints. At least one-third of the foot should be in the stirrup so the rider won't stiffen his ankle in an effort not to lose it; a stiffness, incidentally, resultant also from exaggerated pressing down of the heel. I have found for myself an intermediate position, not quite at the first third of the foot, not all the way back.

Correct leg position.

Incorrect leg position.

There are three different ways to weigh on your stirrups—with the whole foot flat on the floor; principally on the fourth and fifth toes; principally on the big. The third is best, giving your legs effortless contact with the horse's flanks and your calves tautness without muscular contraction. Offset stirrups are fine here. The first manner is acceptable; the second is of course bad, since it counteracts whatever the third promotes.

At a canter, the angles of the (hip, knee, ankle) joints play the rôles of shock absorbers, opening and closing, while the saddle alternately approaches and recedes from the seat. The upper body's forward and the legs' backward slant keep the rider from staying behind, as the force of inertia would cause him to do, were the upper body straight and the legs not "pushing" forward.

Ride as short as you wish, provided it impairs neither your seat, nor the efficiency of your legs. Taking your *manège* riding length for a starting point (stirrup floor at ankle level when the legs drop of their own weight), shorten by four to six holes and let subsequent practice make you find your proper notch.

The Jump of the Horse

Now let us venture to the jump which, remember, is made up of the STRIKE-OFF (first forefeet, then hind feet); the actual TAKE-OFF; the SUSPENSION; the LANDING; and the RECEPTION (like the strike-off, first fore, then hind feet).

STRIKE-OFF OF THE FOREFEET. The horse approaches the obstacle, neck stretched downward, bracing himself like a man preparing to high-jump, then raises head and neck, forelegs reaching successively into the strike-off. As the forelegs leave the ground, the hind feet are set down just about where the forefeet had been, placing the horse practically upright in front of the obstacle. The forelegs are brought close to the body by the simultaneous, if opposite, bending of elbows and knees.

STRIKE-OFF OF THE HIND FEET. While the horse raises his forehand, the hind legs, bent, are on the ground. This bending is prompted by engagement produced when the forefeet strike off and the forehand rises; the release of the hind legs triggers the horse's take-off.

TAKE-OFF. The horse has left the ground and the release of the hind legs has touched off an upward acceleration of his body.

At this moment the neck lengthens and rounds itself through the downward direction of the head, the moment when the horse is at his tautest.

SUSPENSION. Now the horse is horizontally above the obstacle, completely stretched out; his top line is, or should be, slightly incurved, though certain horses, who fail properly to raise their shoulders or to employ their necks, jump hollow and have to expend a far greater effort over the same obstacle than if they wrapped themselves around it.

LANDING. The raising of neck and head marks the beginning of the landing. The forelegs, till now bent, start to stretch toward the ground, the shoulders come down, the quarters pass the obstacle bascule-style.

RECEPTION. The horse touches down on one forefoot, the second following closely; the neck and head descend in order to alleviate the muscles and joints of the forelegs which absorb the impact. The hind legs have passed the obstacle, touching down, one by one, and the horse goes back into a normal canter.

This much for the horse.

The following series of fifteen photos was taken by John Biele at Cherry Meadow Farm, Long Island. While they do not represent the various phases of one and the same jump, they distinctly show the horse's successive gestures before, during and after clearing a fence.

The rider's position (chosen for, rather than despite, its deficiencies) helps us to underscore a number of the most common faults committed just before and during take-off, not only, as do most illustrations, during suspension.

The horse "crouches" before going into the strike-off of the forelegs. The rider is close to the saddle, upper body inclined forward. His hands are, wrongly, leaning on the neck and the reins are slightly slack. This fault would have been avoided had the elbow joints remained supple and the elbows themselves been spread to allow the body to advance through the force of inertia, without altering rein tension.

The instant between the strike-offs of fore and hind legs. The hind legs are about to touch down just behind the spot being vacated by the forelegs. The forehand starts to rise. The rider's hands are a bit too forward, the reins too short, the toe somewhat too much turned out; but the leg is at its place, the stirrup leather at its middle incurved around the leg.

The forelegs have left the ground, the hind legs are still partly bent. By their release they propel the horse upward and forward. Since the horse is very small (14 hands 2), the rider is hard put to place his body, thus leaning sideways, his back rounded, because he is not looking straight ahead. The reins are too short, the heel up.

The situation is ostensibly like the preceding one. Though the hind legs have not yet left the ground, they have already propelled the whole farther up and forward. The remarks concerning the rider are the same as for the preceding photograph.

The hind legs have finished their release and are about to leave the ground. The forelegs are tucked in and above the fence. The rider's reins are too short and the toe is now definitely turned out too much.

The hind legs are leaving the ground, the forelegs have cleared the fence but are still bent. The top line is taut and slightly convex. The reins are too short and the horse does not stretch his neck; the heel is somewhat up, though the leg has remained in place. The remarks concerning the rider's upper body are the same as for the third photo in this series.

The horse starts into the bascule-movement around the fence. The forelegs start to stretch, the top line is rounded; the rider is looking at the next obstacle; his reins are still a little short.

This is another, larger horse, and so the rider is more at ease. The trajectory of the jump is wider, the obstacle being an oxer. The neck extends, the rider is very close to his mount, "going with" the movement. The hands, placed on either side of the neck, are supple and relaxed, letting the reins slide to the extent the horse requires, yet without loss of contact. The legs are at their place, the foot horizontal.

This follows closely the preceding attitude. The horse starts to tuck his hind legs under to let them clear the fence. The trajectory of the jump is very wide because the horse has taken it standing off. The surprised rider is trying to "follow" as best he can. Good neck extension.

The obstacle is higher and wider. Though the hind legs are bent more than on the preceding photo, the forelegs have not gone as far in their trajectory. The rider is a little high over his horse and the heel is going up too much. Though the angle of this shot is not very felicitous, we can see the fine neck extension without the rider losing contact with the mouth.

The hind legs are ready to clear, the forelegs start stretching; the end of suspension and the beginning of the descent. The rider is very close to the saddle, in pliant correspondence with the movement. The supply spread elbows allow for free neck extension, the contact is maintained. The leg has slid back enough literally to push the rider forward, permitting him to remain with his horse rather than fall behind.

The descending phase. The forelegs descend toward the ground, the horse is raising his neck, the hind legs rise over the bar. Through the force of inertia the rider's upper body starts to straighten up.

The hind legs have cleared the pole. The forelegs are completely stretched out and the horse is getting ready to touch down (in this photo) on the near fore. Accentuated elevation of the neck.

The horse has touched down on one fore, the second is about to do so. The hind legs start to descend. The neck is clearly raised. The rider's upper body has been almost completely straightened through the force of inertia, the legs are back at their normal place.

Both forelegs are on the ground, the hind legs are descending, the rider has once more made contact with the hollow of his saddle. As soon as the hind legs touch down, the canter will be resumed. The contact with the mouth has been safeguarded and the rider will be able easily and smoothly to direct his horse toward the next fence.

The Jump of the Rider

Now what about the rider? Approaching the obstacle in the position defined, he leans forward from STRIKE-OFF of the forefeet through TAKE-OFF. The inclination is caused by two facts: the force of inertia, and the rider's gesture of approach to the horse, combined with the horse's own gesture as his forehand rises. Indeed, at the moment of the strike-off of the forefeet a slow-down of the gait draws the rider's upper body forward by the force of inertia. Leaning forward, he draws close to the horse, leaving the hollow of the saddle to alleviate the back and loins and approaching his own center of gravity to that of the horse. During the flexing of knee and ankle joints, his weight diminishes, alleviating the back of his mount, and increases during their extension, a fact you may check on your bathroom scale. Though eventually he is slightly in advance of his horse, he should on no account lean forward prematurely but wait till the horse initiates the jump.

At the TAKE-OFF he will then be slightly ahead of his horse, as he must if he wishes to be with him during suspension, the extreme inclination of his upper body letting him keep ahead in the motion of the jump.

At the moment of SUSPENSION, however, the horse has caught up and both are moving together, the rider holding up his head and looking at the next obstacle, the legs maintaining their backward slant, the hands resting on the neck, forward of the withers.

At the LANDING the rider lags behind, descending more slowly than the horse. Thighs and knees slide somewhat back and up, taking along legs and feet, the latter losing pressure on, and sometimes contact with, the stirrups. The upper body straightens up by itself through the force of inertia.

The Jump Saddle

While clothes do not make the man and tack does not make the horseman, a horse show saddle must for efficiency's sake meet certain requirements: be light, simple and supple, with flaps sufficiently advanced to accommodate the knees without the need to sit farther back; knee-rolls and leather blocks so placed as to afford a proper grip, without it looking like an orthopedic saddle. The knee-rolls, at the front, are attached to the sweat-flaps, level with the bottoms of the thighs, just above the knees. The leather blocks, far back on the sweat-flaps, are placed just below the backs of the knees and just above the calves. The pad, usually made of felt, is not really such a blessing, since it interposes itself between horse and rider, impairs the efficiency of the legs and, unless in impeccable condition, may injure the horse. Its dubious popularity comes from the fact that, to the detriment of horse and saddle, it saves a lot of glycerin-soap and elbow-grease otherwise expended on the panels. But a saddle should be done thoroughly every day after dismounting; and "doing a saddle" means cleaning it with preferably lukewarm water, a sponge and a bunch of horsehair to take the dirt and dried sweat off the panels and sweat-flaps before spreading the glycerin-soap with the sponge, massaging the soap in to keep the leather supple.

Flat and hollow-seated saddles with advanced flaps.

CHAPTER THREE

Preparatory Exercises

Although it is hoped that our pupil comes to his first jumping lessons equipped with the rudiments of equitation, a reasonably good seat and some steadiness, still he seldom gets to feel his stirrups while we exercise him further to improve his seat, condition him to the reflex of opening his fingers rather than closing them over the jump—that is, to respect his horse's mouth—and teach him pliancy at a trot, at a canter and over small, calmly taken obstacles.

Special stress is laid on *calm*, because the rider's morale, just as important as the horse's, will be the decisive factor in the show ring. You sometimes see a bunch of competitors, inspecting a rather easy course, stop to gaze worriedly at a combination jump composed of, say, a straight fence and an oxer. It is the distance between its two elements and the makeup of the second which makes it look forbidding, and the first entry promptly commits a big fault at the oxer. The second does the same and every subsequent one does, if possible, worse, till the turn comes for the ubiquitous maverick who thinks he's got the key to the problem. "Letting his horse do it," he approaches the jump at increasing speed, clears it faultlessly and with an air of ease. Lo and behold! only one thereafter commits a fault there. What has happened?

My guess is that everybody was a bit shaken, vaguely thinking something would have to be done at that point and vaguely proceeding to vaguely do it; hardly an attitude to inspire a horse who, under only the vaguest impulsion, either refused at the first or faulted at the second.

"Go with a will and let me do it," rumor has the horses tell their riders at Saumur. If this advice is unsurpassed for the neophyte at the obstacle, it does not lack merit for the experienced horseman who reads between its lines a definition of the problem of the jump. The will to do is the readiness to pass, and being prepared to pass means to arrive with a balanced horse with good impulsion, proper engagement and speed, to be able to lead him to the best spot for the take-off and to convey to him one's own will to conquer. The "let me do it" part is no less applicable to both. Since initiative on the part of an inexperienced rider is liable to handicap his horse, the best he can do is play dead on his back and follow him. He sets him in the right direction and takes care of impulsion, and the instinct and experience of the "beginner's horse" he should be riding—by definition anything but a beginner himself—will safely solve the problems of the jump for both. Though the experienced rider does of course give indications to his horse—advice rather than command—concerning lengthening or shortening of stride, increased engagement for maximum power, still the horse is the one who jumps, and at the moment of the take-off his rider should but follow, making himself as unobtrusive as he can.

The following then are exercises to develop seat, steadiness, and respect for the mouth of a horse who has to fear, at the moment of the jump, not only the weight of our body but the even heavier one of our hand. By the time he enters competition, your pupil must be able to maintain his steadiness, even when surprised by an early take-off, sure his fingers will give the horse all the neck he might require and request in order to get out of a difficult situation. Though meaningless *per se*, these exercises are to the show rider what scales are to the pianist: no more, no less. than a necessity. Their usefulness is material as well as psychological, because they allow him to break up and conquer the difficulties one by one before having to cope with the following. They let the rider in his training, not unlike the horse in his own, explore the mechanism of the jump at work, assimilate it in slow motion, till, once the good reflexes have settled in, he can duplicate the performance more quickly on the course. This process naturally requires calm, order, and trained—that is, eager and quiet—horses.

Four Exercises

For the management exercises of the first half of each lesson our student uses the stirrups. During the second, when he drops them, he is spared needless fatigue by staying at a walk, except for the actual jumping exercises which are as follows:

FIRST EXERCISE. Poles on ground level on the track discard all problems of management, so that—hands low, reins long—all the pupil has to worry about is seat. Once relaxed and somewhat steady, he does the same exercise with simultaneous (backward) arm and head rotation. If the glance follows the hand as it should, he cannot watch his horse and, taken unawares when the horse steps across the pole, his loins can absorb the shock only if they are consistently relaxed.

SECOND EXERCISE. The same, but over 1½ ft, where the reactions are stronger and the loins must be even more supple. We might add a few small oxers, same height, 2 ft wide. Though we use both trot and canter, stress is placed on the trot. When seat no longer seems to be a major problem and the pupil has suppleness and steadiness and keeps his hands low, we let him take the reins again, though the obstacles remain on the track. First at our prompting, then by himself, he will open his fingers and, without raising his hands, let the reins slip at the moment of the jump.

THIRD EXERCISE. This should not be done before the other two are executed easily and correctly. We now take the poles off the track and scatter them through the school in such a way that direction must be changed after each. The difficulties of management, gradually increased, are keeping step with progress. If the progression has been rational, all should go smoothly, since this exercise is really but a combination of previous practice; i.e., management on the flat and jumping on the track.

In all three exercises the rider remains in the saddle, without stirrups, at a trot and at a canter, so that, wishing to absorb the reactions, he must lean back at the moment of the jump and thereby let the reins slip between his fingers.

FOURTH EXERCISE. Meanwhile we have taught the POSTING TROT WITHOUT STIRRUPS. Position does not change from the posting trot with stirrups, toes pointing up.

The same obstacles are taken, still without stirrups, but leaning forward. At a trot he is, since he is posting, already in the right jumping position, placing his hands on each side of the neck at the moment of the jump. At a canter, he remains in the saddle and leans forward at the jump.

When these four exercises come easily, the stirrups may be taken up, sure our seat is good enough to follow the horse without having to hang on to the reins, though we will intermittently go back to this work. In the meantime we practice on the flat, at a trot and at a canter, holding the position of the rider on the course as defined, in balance on the stirrups. Once this is done without difficulty on the flat, single obstacles are taken, posing several simultaneous problems: direction, impulsion and speed first; engagement, balance, lengthening and shortening of stride later. The one problem we have by now solved is seat; our reflexes have taken root.

CHAPTER FOUR

Direction, Impulsion and Speed

D IRECTION is given by way of rein effects in combination with leg action. We shall briefly recapitulate these aids.

The Five Rein Effects

1. THE OPENING REIN (1st effect) has a natural action upon the horse. It consists of drawing his nose in the direction one wants to take.

To turn right, make your right wrist pivot right a quarter of a turn, thereby turning your nails up, and shift it to the right, keeping your elbows close to the body.

2. THE COUNTER-REIN (2nd effect), also called the NECK REIN, acts upon the base of the neck which it nudges in the proposed direction.

To turn right, make your left wrist act from left to right and from back to front. It is the only rein effect permitting you to manage your horse with a single hand. Unlike the opening rein, the horse, able to evade it without trouble, must be trained to obey it.

BOTH REIN EFFECTS act on the forehand that takes the new direction, while the hindquarters are content to follow the shoulders in this change. Since the action does not interfere with the forward movement, the result does not incite the horse to slow down.

The following three rein effects, on the contrary, address the hindquarters. By a rational disposition of his reins, the rider OPPOSES THE SHOULDERS TO THE HAUNCHES, whence their appellation of REINS OF OPPOSITION. Now, this opposition impairs the forward movement which the rider's legs must painstakingly keep intact or restore whenever it tends to disappear; and the effectiveness of these reins is commensurate with the degree of activity the rider creates in the hindquarters.

3. THE DIRECT REIN OF OPPOSITION acts upon the HAUNCHES.

4. THE COUNTER-REIN OF OPPOSITION IN FRONT OF THE WITHERS (4th effect) acts upon the SHOULDERS.

5. THE COUNTER-REIN OF OPPOSITION BEHIND THE WITHERS (5th effect or INTERMEDIATE REIN) acts upon the SHOULDERS AND THE HAUNCHES.

In performing THE RIGHT DIRECT REIN OF OPPOSITION —which makes the horse turn right by pushing his haunches to the left—the rider tightens the right rein in the direction of his right knee, after slightly relaxing the fingers of his left hand so as to make the horse understand more easily the action of the right. With this effect the reins remain parallel to the horse's axis.

In performing THE RIGHT COUNTER-REIN OF OPPOSITION IN FRONT OF THE WITHERS—which makes the horse turn left by throwing his shoulders to the left and his haunches to the right, the horse thus pivoting around an axis passing approximately through the vertical of the stirrup leathers—the rider, increasing finger pressure on the right rein, shifts his right wrist in a leftward direction, so that an imaginary line, continuing in this direction, would pass in front of the withers. Only this way may we, of course, understand this term, "in front of the withers," and the following, "behind the withers."

Since THE RIGHT COUNTER-REIN OF OPPOSITION BEHIND THE WITHERS displaces the whole horse toward the left —this rein effect being INTERMEDIATE between the direct rein of opposition, which only acts upon the haunches, and the counter-rein of opposition in front of the withers, which only acts upon the shoulders—it falls to the rider, in shifting his right wrist toward the left, to determine how far behind the withers the right rein should pass in order to act with equal intensity upon shoulders and haunches; because the more this intermediate rein tends to approach the direct rein of opposition, the more it acts upon the hindquarters; and, on the contrary, the more it tends to approach the counter-rein of opposition in front of the withers, the greater its effect on the forehand.

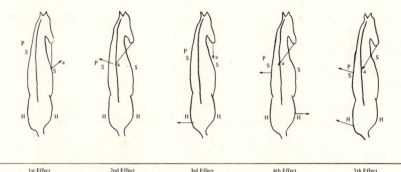

| 1st Effect | 2nd Effect | 3rd Effect | 4th Effect | 5th Effect |

The Five Rein Effects. "a" represents the active hand, "p" the passive hand, "S" the shoulders, and "H" the haunches.

The following chart gives you an example of THE COORDI-NATION OF THE AIDS and sums up THE FIVE REIN EFFECTS, showing, by means of THE ACTION OF THE LEG reinforcing them, the meaning of THE LATERAL AND DIAGONAL AIDS; *lateral aids* being the combination of the hand and leg acting on the same side (example: the right hand and leg are the *right lateral aids*), *diagonal aids* being the combination of the hand of one side and the leg of the opposite (example: the left hand and right leg).

Of the five rein effects, the *Direct Rein of Opposition* and the *Fourth Effect* are of the most frequent practical use.

The direct rein of opposition, because the easiest, is particularly recommended for the beginner. In order to avoid all traction on the mouth, he must be accustomed to yielding with the outside hand (right when turning left) and to resisting, no more, with the inside hand.

The fourth effect is used specifically on short turns where, particularly if the jump comes at the end of the turn, the outside leg (left on a right curve) must be applied to the flank so as to hold the haunches, at least limit their shift, and maintain the engagement of the hind legs.

At all events, and this is important, the head is held high and the eyes set on the jump or in the direction to be taken.

APPLICATION OF THE COORDINATION OF THE AIDS

Acting Rein	Forehand	Acting Leg	Hindquarters	New Direction Taken	Aids Applied
I. Right opening rein	Drawn to the right	Right, pushing the haunches to the left, aiding the right turn.	Pushed to the left	To the right	Lateral*
II. Right counter-rein	Pushed to the left	Left, pushing the haunches to the right, aiding the left turn.	Pushed to the right	To the left	Diagonal**
III. Right direct rein of opposition	Turned to the right	Right, reinforcing the action of the right rein which pushes the haunches to the left.	Pushed to the left	To the right	Lateral
IV. Right counter-rein of opposition in front of the withers; 4th effect	Pushed to the left	Left, reinforcing the action of the right rein which pushes the haunches to the right.	Pushed to the right	To the left	Diagonal
V. Right counter-rein of opposition behind the withers; 5th effect or intermediate rein	Pushed to the left	Right, reinforcing the action of the right rein which pushes the haunches to the left.	Pushed to the left	The entire horse is moved to the left.	Lateral

* One calls lateral aids the combination of the hand and leg acting on the same side. Example: The right hand and leg are the right lateral aids.

** One calls diagonal aids the combination of the hand of one side and the leg of the opposite. Example: The left hand and right leg.

IMPULSION is created by the legs and stored, channeled, liberated through the hands; and if we want to keep an impulsive reserve and thereby a taut horse, hand and leg action must be commensurate.

SPEED, for beginners, should be held down conveniently; that is, to a minimum.

Schooling over Singles

Our exercises will now take place over eight or ten single fences, 2½ ft high. After each jump we check to a walk and at this gait take our horse to about 15 yards from the following, where we request another strike-off into the canter, jump, and immediately recheck to a walk, and so on. During the jump the hands rest on each side of the neck, forward of the withers. This way the shoulders and arms yield sufficiently so as not to require the fingers to let the reins slip. The rider must then and there learn to keep contact with the horse's mouth during the jump; for there is nothing harder or more delicate than retaking contact.

During the same exercise we then check to a trot between jumps, till we finally make the entire round at a canter, though slowing down between jumps and applying ourselves to guiding our horse straight toward the center of the next obstacle. If the rider feels his horse float or hesitate, all he can do is leave his hands in place, sit down in the saddle and use his legs to drive him back onto the bit. Watch the speed; whenever a horse speeds up on his own, eight times out of ten he means to refuse or to run out. So let us avoid speed for now and try to maintain an even pace on our little courses.

The aim of all these exercises is to teach the proper use of legs and hands, control and management from a good position on an easy course. It is up to you, the instructor, to keep out any horse that rushes at his fences, refuses or runs out.

So let us not rush at our fences either, but remember that the more we try to hurry, the more time we shall lose. Alas, haste is only too common; instructors let beginners freewheel over the fences, without teaching them, as soon as they have a minimum of steadiness, efficient use of legs and hands and to sit down in the saddle any time additional effectiveness of aids is required.

We should vary the obstacles as much as possible up to 3 or 3½ ft, not necessarily all of them maximum height, including easy doubles two strides wide. If well built, they are not complicated, less so if our pupil makes their acquaintance jumping them three or four times on the outer track where the wall or fence serves as a ramp; for at the end of this period there usually comes our first horse show.

CHAPTER FIVE

The First Horse Show

N ot one of those popular events where in a small, fenced-in ring all obstacles save one or two are lined up along the outer track. This, by the way, is fine for training children, but I am speaking here of a 3 to 3½ ft course requiring a little management. Needless to say we choose only classes amply within horse's and rider's capabilities and, once our mind is made up, do not miss the last entry date. We make sure well before the day has come that the horse will enter the van without a fuss and then carry knee-caps, poll bumpers (by all means if the van is small), stable bandages with thick cotton layers, a lambskin-lined halter, a tail guard and a blanket or sheet, as the season warrants. We have checked the shoes four or five days earlier, so that, if reshoeing is necessary, the horse has that many days to get used to the new. If the course is turf, we calk; if not, we still should have the outer edges slightly turned up at the heels of the hind feet. Though we have made sure that all is well with our tack, we take along an extra girth, a pair of stirrup leathers and two extra reins. We have inquired where on location we can find bedding, oats and hay and are carrying two canvas pails, one for drinking, the other for tack cleaning and grooming.

On the eve of the horse show—or, if the event is at a distance, of the shipping—the horse is worked normally, jumping four or five poles at the end of the lesson and, if at all possible, taken for a quiet ride at slow gaits, mostly at a walk. It is not on the last day that anything new can be taught or learned; and anyway, we are

c

having to do with a *beginning rider* and a *well-versed, not to say aged, horse* who knows this kind of work by heart. Since any of those first events are easy, we need not bring our horse gradually up to top form for it and had better try not to make him sick and tired of taking endless fences during the last days prior to the show.

If distance causes us to arrive the day before the event, we work calmly at the three gaits for about an hour, dodging the frantic horseman one finds in any exercise ring, who "canters off in all directions" at top speed, taking and retaking ever higher trial bars.

As soon as our class has been posted, we study the course attentively, memorize it, then do it in our head. If we can, we pace off the actual course, passing exactly where we will with our horse, choosing well where to turn to best approach each subsequent jump. If we can, I said, because, regrettably, course inspection has not been generally permitted in this country, though it makes for smoother performances by giving the riders advance knowledge of the difficulties and a chance to plan accordingly, although it is startling to see them allowed to ride around the course during the setting up of fences, letting their horses see and sniff and jump those which might cause them concern.

If our place on the entry list allows us to see the rounds of a number of riders before us, we watch them, by all means; it may tell us something. But we need about half an hour to limber up the horse before our own turn, above all at a trot, speed-ups, slow-downs, a few strike-offs from the walk into the canter, halts, rein-backs, in the end three or four calm jumps of the trial bar. Whatever time remains, we wait it out at a walk and trot.

Entering the arena at a trot, we salute the judges, make a volte during which we strike off into the canter on the proper lead for the first turn (left curve, left lead). Reins rather short, we go straight and at a normal speed to the first obstacle. Even if our horse is keen and generous, we do not leave things up to him but take him well into our legs between jumps. If we feel him nicely on the bit, going to it eagerly, we need not pummel him with our heels, just keep him aware that our legs are active *in accord with the cadence*, and that we are not a dead weight on his back. If we sense him hesitate, not respond as he should to the action of our legs, or if he tries to drop the bit, we sit down in the saddle, from where our aids will be much more effective. If able to maintain a rational pace, we need not halt or check between jumps, rather

too obviously the way of an elementary rider or an insufficiently
schooled mount. Besides, it makes the course that much harder for
the horse, physically and morally, wastes a lot of time, an important
factor in later events where time will count, and robs the round
of smoothness and grace. This kind of thing, though hard on the
hocks, is useful to a point in jumping single obstacles, but not
on a course with doubles and trebles. Let us not get into the habit
of the motorized speed bugs who, rather than ease up on the accelerator in time to take a steep turn, slam on the brake, then hit the
accelerator again. Poor engine, poor passenger.

Our round is finished. No matter how it went, we never hasten
to conclusions. We still have a great deal to learn, and will, provided we know how to use what such shows can teach us: listening
carefully and objectively to all comments on our own performance,
watching those of others, remembering and analyzing what we
have done or should have done. Though at this level chance still
plays a major part, all is not just good or bad luck. We should
develop an early skill for prospective and retrospective analysis of
our rounds and learn to draw conclusions. One conclusion we should
never draw from winning a class is that all was perfect. If we objectively single out the poorer parts of our performance and are
able to clearly distinguish between what we did and should have
done, we can try to apply any new solutions another time under
similar circumstances; should they prove false, never mind! it is
the only way to make progress.

CHAPTER SIX

Speed-Ups, Slow-Downs and Balance

The exercises in the school, schooling over the fences and a few horse shows have given us a certain routine, so that steering a trained, experienced horse over simple courses of 3 to 3½ ft is no longer a problem. In the process we have developed enough equestrian tact to tackle new difficulties.

On a trained horse (and such is the case with us) the rider without physical exertion is able to speed up or slow the gait by lengthening or shortening the strides. If during the speed-up *the reins stay tight enough*—fingers and wrists accompanying neck and head movements with such precision that rein tension never varies in permitting and encouraging this speed-up prompted by the legs —the horse will keep his hind legs engaged, because the speed-up is obtained by an increase in leg action, not only by an opening of fingers. The horse remains taut, a matter of dosage in leg and hand action.

Slow-downs require no less concern for the maintenance or increase of the engagement of the hind legs. The hands should not busy themselves continuously but in short successive actions till the desired slow-down is reached. Here too all is in the dosage, the legs intervening as necessary, alternating with the hands, if the horse is to remain taut.

If we are able to speed up and slow down while keeping control of the engagement we are able to control the balance. *But at the base of this scaffolding there is IMPULSION. With it, speed variations, the control of engagement and balance are possible; without it, they become purely and simply impossible.*

Speed-ups and Slow-downs

We begin on the flat. A speed-up at the canter, at first by a maximum yielding of the hands, putting the horse into a void. Gradual leg intervention renders the speed-up gradual enough to give our pupil time to feel the different changes of balance produced. Then we ask him not only to keep his legs quite passive but to spread them slightly, away from contact with the horse, while tightening the reins progressively and continuously till the canter is broken. What happens?

IN THE SPEED-UP the legs increase the impulsion which, no longer channeled and stored by the hands, degenerates into speed; the horse no longer taut, the hind legs not engaged, the balance escapes toward the front.

IN THE SLOW-DOWN the hands increase rein tension, obtaining the desired slow-down; but with legs totally inactive, the impulsion vanishes bit by bit through the action of the hands. The horse is not taut, the hind legs are not engaged, the balance remains in the front.

This extreme example of the worst that can happen lets the pupil best understand and feel the collaborative pattern of hand and leg action; it teaches him to realize when things start to go wrong and to straighten them out before it is too late.

This is the art of horsemanship: to know how to graduate and combine the aids at the right moment, just when the need is felt. Of course, such actions become fewer and less obvious as the horseman's sensitivity increases, since his aids *maintain*, rather than *set*, the horse "right."

Balance

Proceeding from this exercise, always through a rational progression, we develop our pupil's sense of balance. Working at a canter of 350 to 400 yards per minute, we request slow-downs and speed-ups by alternate leg and hand action, shunning excessive changes of balance, limiting the speed-ups and the slow-downs as well, so as not to tamper with impulsion.

Once these speed-ups and slow-downs come easily and, above all, the rider *feels* what is going on under him, has acquired a feel for pace and balance, we are ready to cope with the problem of strides. In progression these stages are close together, not so in time. Only long practice and experience will lead to all this; and the instructor's help and guidance, no matter how good, cannot possibly take their place.

The normal stride of a horse standing 16 hands is about 10 ft; but the rider can lengthen or shorten it.

TO LENGTHEN STRIDE the legs must act and the hands accompany the motion of neck and head, both hands and legs *respecting the cadence* of the gait. For a further increase of leg action we sit down in the saddle and make use of our seat.

TO SHORTEN STRIDE, always *respecting the cadence,* we take the horse in at every stride, and this at the first time (one hind leg firmly on the ground, the forelegs in the air). The pupil gets used to judging distance by pinpointing guide marks along the walls of the ring, then covering a given distance in a varying number of strides by shortening or lengthening them.

Knowing how to do this is a fine thing for several reasons:

1. Shortening of strides is particularly interesting in that it obtains a greater engagement of the hind legs, thus modifying balance; the quarters take on additional weight, relieving the forehand by as much, and store excess impulsion to be released at the moment of the jump. The inherent danger lies in loss of speed.

2. Lengthening of strides is fine for increasing speed, but if done indiscriminately is liable to set the horse on the shoulders.

3. Choice can be exercised depending on the kind of horse one is riding.

4. For combinations (doubles and trebles) it is important, yea essential, to be able to shorten or lengthen the last strides at will.

5. It capacitates the rider to lead his horse to the best place for the take-off.

Ultimately the choice depends on several variable factors which must be considered jointly, to wit:

1. The shortening by combined but not simultaneous action of legs and hands causes the horse to further engage his hind legs. Rein tension, though increased, must not be continuous and uniform. The hands always accompany the motion of head and neck, though not in their full scope, encouraging and stimulating the forward movement, while limiting the length of the strides. Let us look upon the horse as a spring compressed between your hands and legs; and now imagine such a spiral spring compressed between your hands: At first the left offers but weak resistance, letting itself be nudged to the left by the pushing of the right. As the pushing of the right increases—the left increasing its resistance too but still letting itself be shifted to the left—the spring will become ever tauter, without the left hand ceasing to shift to the left. This is the essence of a problem your hands and legs solve with more or less felicity according to your talents. Alas, this way of doing slows you down; just as in lengthening strides, you must not go beyond a certain limit and be sure your horse responds perfectly to your leg action. Aside from this purely physical side, there is the more abstract of guessing your horse's impressions and knowing how to convey your own to him. He can be made to concentrate as well as you, and only if you understand and use him accordingly can you take advantage of both his innate and acquired resources.

2. The lengthening of strides lets you approach the obstacle at increasing speed, essential when you must cover a spread jump right up to the limits of your horse's capacities. Approaching a double or treble with a somewhat sluggish horse, you had better do so with a lengthening of the last strides, allowing him to make maximum use of his speed to dominate the obstacle. Sometimes, of course, an interior distance or the nature of the component parts will make you opt for an approach by short strides. Furthermore, if approaching the first obstacle you have reached the maximum speed *permissible*, a further speed-up might set your horse on his shoulders and make him start off all wrong. Catastrophe ensues; you simply cannot afford a mistake. The worst, however, is the horse that "slips along." To avoid this, our hands "permitting" what the legs "request," we hold back just enough to arrive with some reserve impulsion, the more so when dealing with a double or treble. In classes where the stop watch counts we can gain time by lengthening the last strides and standing off more at a vertical, but unless we have a submissive and calm horse on a suitable course, we lose, rather than gain, time this way. At times it is best to take

an extra stride and turn short after the obstacle, rather than have the stride we gain force us into a wide turn.

3. The behavior, character and capacities of our horse are points to ponder. Avoid long strides with a horse poorly balanced by nature; they might set him on his shoulders. Avoid them with the horse who tends to go too fast, because after the jump you may be hard put to check him, lack the time to prepare him for the following obstacle or to make him turn as he should. But with a well-balanced horse that needs some urging, you do well to approach the jump at long strides. The well-schooled horse is the one that can be led at long or short strides, the choice depending entirely on the obstacle or combination before us.

4. This choice, with combinations, is discussed in the chapter on doubles and trebles.

5. The kind of horse and obstacle determines the best place for our take-off. This is where the horse must be led, here or as hard by as possible. This is the spot where the forefeet will strike off. The strike off, too, may be called short or long by association, depending on its distance from the obstacle. At any rate, we should strike off "right," because doing so the horse wraps himself around the jump, expending a minimum of effort. Standing off, he goes like an arrow; getting under, he jumps with a hollow back. Where must we, then, take off in order to be "right"? It is a complex question best answered by example.

Over a 4-ft. obstacle most horses cover 9 to 18 ft. from take-off to landing. If the summit of the trajectory is above that of the obstacle, the distances from take-off to the foot of the obstacle and from the foot to the landing are equal, that is, 4 ft. 6 ins. to 9 ft. Thus the best spot for the take-off is between 4 ft. 6 ins. and 9 ft. The minimum distance for a normal jump, incidentally, is about equal to the height of the obstacle. If closer, the horse is liable to commit a fault, unless, extremely wary of touching, he makes an effort out of all proportion to the obstacle.

Once we are on horseback inside an arena, this kind of mathematics loses, of course, some of its applicability. The way our horse jumps will then be conditioned by his speed of approach to the fence, his balance, his size, and, last not least, his form. I have known a very small horse (really a pony but for an inch) to cover 15 ft. when leading up at long strides to a 3 ft. 6 ins. vertical, not once, but on the average.

To get closer to the foot of the obstacle we diminish, to take off from far we increase rein tension. A helpful trick for practice is to look at its foot in the first, at its summit in the second case; but it obviously is nothing but a trick and not even a magic one: the rider's general attitude is influenced by his glance and communicates itself, in turn, to the horse through the use of the aids.

Still, our pupil will be quite hesitant as to his choice in every case. The compromise solution is, before requesting the lengthening of the last strides, to get our horse "reorganized" by shortening the strides (engagement of the hind legs, rebalancing), then ride him strongly by long strides to the right place. This solution seems ideal but requires a well-schooled (i.e., submissive) horse and a tactful rider, since the reorganizing must be done quickly and without brusqueness, spelling disaster if the horse does not respond quickly and submissively to light hand action.

Let us wind this up with a few examples which may stand in apparent, but only apparent, contradiction. "Getting there by long strides saves time," one book tells us; another says, "short strides gain time;" others maintain that "with the horse in need of pushing we go fast." They are right, one and all, depending on the style and temperament of horse and rider. If we cannot canter fast because the horse is hard to hold beyond a certain limit or because, beyond his natural pace, he becomes disorganized, we had better arrive without too much speed and lengthen only the last few strides. If, on the contrary, we have a very skillful, submissive horse we know well, we can, to gain time, take him beyond his natural pace between obstacles, approaching each at short strides, which enables us to rebalance him. "Going fast with a horse in need of pushing" means that this kind of horse will never try to go too fast by himself, or even beyond his normal speed. Therefore, master absolute of speed, the rider can turn, if necessary, very short, lengthen the last strides or speed up between two obstacles. It is, above all, a question of schooling, the best possible use of our and the horse's natural qualities; and, of course, the longer both have worked together the more successful the combination is bound to be.

What really counts is "to ride as one feels" and to know the why and how of all one does. Placing the strike-off just where one wants it to occur is already on a level we cannot reach before we have solved the problems of impulsion, engagement, balance, speed and direction. What use taking our horse to the ideal spot for the take-off with a faulty balance?

CHAPTER EIGHT

Doubles, Trebles, Water Jumps and Banks

Doubles and trebles are on the whole not quite as complicated as people tend to think. The worst are built by mediocre course architects, their built-in hardships impossibilities only blind luck can overcome.

The component parts of such a combination must have considerable frontage (16 to 18 ft.), be well-aligned, massive and inviting. The worst are composed of poles too light and few, letting the following fence, built along just about the same lines, show through. In this optical confusion without a firm background, the horse arriving at a canter cannot quite tell which poles belong to which.

Though there are no absolute rules, a double is usually composed of a straight and a spread fence, or vice versa; a treble will have two spread fences framing a straight, or two straight fences framing a spread.

The straight fences include walls; obstacles made of poles or gates with and without brush, on the same vertical plane.

The spread fences include oxers; *barres en A*; triple bars; water jumps and brooks.

THE OXER is a spread fence composed of two elements. It may be *square*, both elements of equal height, also equal to the width of the whole obstacle. It may be *parallel*, the height of both elements equal, but the width separating them greater or lesser than their height. It may be built in an *ascending* line, the first element lower than the second, the easiest type of oxer to jump.

THE HOG'S BACK, a classic obstacle, though little known in this country, is made up of three poles, two of equally low height, quite far apart, the space in between giving us the width of the obstacle. The third pole, on a higher plane, evenly spaced between them, constitutes the determining height. (See illustration.)

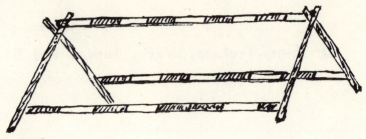

Hog's Back

THE TRIPLE BAR is made up of three evenly spaced poles at progressively rising heights.

THE WATER JUMP AND BROOK may both be open-edged (the most difficult to jump!); in fact, the water jump may at the most have a small hedge on the take-off side, while the brook may have a post and rails or triple bar at its center.

Experience has shown that with two straight fences at a distance of 25 ft. the horse will approach the second properly after one stride of the canter, if the first fence has been taken normally (neither standing off too far, nor getting under). At a 35-ft. distance between the two obstacles the same holds true, the horse taking two strides instead of one. Since this has been proved a thousand times, we may take it for granted with most horses. The difference between 35 and 25 ft. being 10 ft., we arrive at the length of a normal stride of the canter. In the first case (a distance of 25 ft.) one stride equaling 10 ft., we may say that the two half-trajectories within the combination equal 15 ft. If we assume that the horse has correctly taken the first fence (the trajectory properly framing the obstacle, its summit just above that of the obstacle), they are equal; each 7 ft. 6 ins.

The proper distance, thus, for a double composed of two *straight fences* is 25 ft. for one stride, 35 ft. for two. These distances may be reduced or increased by 1 ft. 6 ins. in the first case, 2 ft. to 2 ft. 6 ins. in the second. The problem of long or short distance must be solved on approaching the first fence of the combination. Often the very manner of jumping the obstacle immediately prior to the double is important. Sometimes we should, even while jumping the two or three preceding obstacles, let the combination and the distance separating them therefrom enter in our calculations. One must be horseman enough to know before he starts in on a round what he is going to do at such a point. But we shall return to this later.

If this 25-ft. distance is best for a double composed of two straight fences (applicable also to the 35 ft. distance, the difference embodied in a second stride), things change when the two components are no longer alike. So let us examine the different combinations possible in a double.

Double Whose First Fence Is a Straight

1. If the second also is a straight fence, the proper distance is 25 ft. for one stride.

2. If the second is a square or parallel oxer, the proper distance is the same as for a straight fence, but the oxer must be taken with more impulsion, since the trajectory must be wider than for a straight, on account of the width to be covered.

3. If the second is an ascendant oxer, the proper distance is 24 ft. for one stride. In fact, the first element of the oxer being lower than the second, the horse had better get close to its foot for easy coverage of the width, the summit of the trajectory being slightly in advance of the second element or just above it. This is due to the difference in height of the two elements; the greater the difference, the more the summit of the trajectory tends to pass above the second element; the smaller it is (as with an almost parallel oxer), the more the summit of the trajectory will shift between the two.

4. If the second is a triple bar, the best distance is even less than in the preceding case (23 ft. 6 ins.). The chief problem is covering the obstacle, its width posing a greater challenge than its height. Since the first element is rather low and the forelegs will hardly commit a fault there, we should get as close as possible. The trajectory of the jump is even wider.

Doubles Whose First Fence Is a Square or Parallel Oxer

Though the trajectory over the first obstacle is wider than over a straight fence, the above dimensions, including the observations applying thereto, remain valid for combinations beginning with a square oxer. With a parallel oxer of great width (4 ft. 7 ins. by a width of 5 ft. 3 ins.) the trajectory will be commensurately wider to where it exceeds the norm (15 ft.). In sum, with doubles beginning with an oxer, the distance separating the two fences had better at least equal the one given under the previous heading and preferably exceed it by a few inches.

Doubles Whose First Fence Is an Ascendant Oxer

Jumping the first obstacle, the horse will touch down at a greater distance than above, since the trajectory will on one hand be wider than with a straight fence and its summit, and on the other will be above, or almost above, the second element of the oxer—not between the two elements, as it was with the square and parallel oxers. To remain right, the distance between the two oxers must be increased.

1. If the second obstacle is a straight fence, the proper distance is about 26 ft.

2. If the second obstacle is a square or parallel oxer, the distance is the same as for a straight fence, 26 ft.

3. If the second obstacle is an ascendant oxer, we return to a distance of 25 ft.

4. If the second obstacle is a triple bar, the proper distance is just barely 25 ft.

Doubles Whose First Fence Is a Triple Bar

Here the horse will touch down even farther from the foot of the first fence, and this for the same reason given under the preceding heading (a wider trajectory, this obstacle being even wider than the ascendant oxer, its summit above the third bar). If we want to keep a proper distance, the picture should be as follows:

1. If the second fence is a straight fence, the proper distance is a carefully measured 26 ft. 6 ins.

2. If the second fence is a square or parallel oxer, the distance is the same as for a straight fence.

3. If the second fence is an ascendant oxer, we return to a distance of 26 ft.

4. If the second fence is a triple bar, the distance is even less, preferably 25 ft.

The above leads to the following deductions:

a) When the second fence of a double is of the same nature as the first, regardless of type, the best distance is 25 ft. for one stride;

b) a square oxer (unless a mountain) or parallel oxer (unless a gulf) may be treated like a straight fence, at least as concerns distances;

c) the trajectories of the jumps, at least when normal, vary with the shape of the fences to jump, making the horse touch down at varying distances from their feet.

Distances are measured from the interior face of the foot of the first fence to the interior face of the foot of the second.

We will take the example of a double made up as follows: first fence a parallel oxer 4 ft. 7 ins. by a width of 5 ft. 3 ins.; second fence a 5-ft. straight fence. If the jump over the oxer is regular and normal, the summit of the trajectory will be above, and at equal distances from, the two poles; the horse will land at about 7 ft. 6 in. to 8 ft. from the foot of the obstacle (inside).

Let us now put in the oxer's place a triple bar, its height and width no different from the oxer's. The trajectory will be wider over the triple bar and its summit above the last element of the obstacle. The horse will land farther away. Thus the distance, to remain right, must be increased, though, in our examples of two different combinations, neither height nor width differed.

No chart, of course, no matter how conscientious, will prove infallible. Course architects devise more combinations than the pen can record. Geometry requires not only theorems for the solution of its problems, but a measure of intelligence in their choice and application. Then conclusions must be drawn which lead to the right solutions. Neither here nor there would you want to learn all possible problems by heart; and this little review of doubles only intends to give you the general principles which never fail. The relevant detail is a variable to be determined as the occasion arises.

Two other factors enter into our evaluation of distance on a course: the grounds and your horse's way of cantering and jumping. On turf, firm but elastic, in perfect conditions, the strides will be other than on boggy ground or sand, so, more than anything, the rider must know how his horse canters and jumps. Nothing is as important for him as to be in correspondence to the point of feeling that his horse's legs are his own, that their will is but one, in brief, that they are in absolute communion. To reach this point takes great practice and patience, and even then it does not "click" with one and every horse; if and when this communion is achieved, all our efforts are richly rewarded. There is more to showing than mere mathematics, a frequent aid to be sure, but superseded by our knowledge of our own horse.

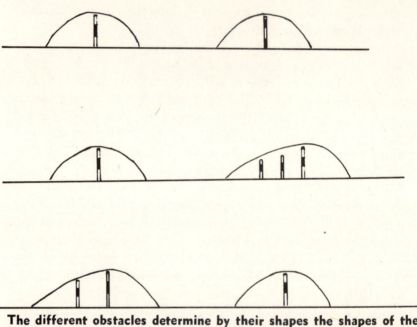

The different obstacles determine by their shapes the shapes of the trajectories. Top: two straight fences; center: one straight fence, one triple bar; bottom: one ascending oxer, one straight fence.

Trebles

At least in theory, the problem is the same as with the doubles, though the distance between the second and third obstacles had better be somewhat less.

Let us take a simple example: a treble composed of three straight fences. We have seen that the best distance is 25 ft. for one stride, 35 ft. for two. This remains valid for the trebles, but in practice the horse does not attack the third obstacle with impulsion, speed or balance equal to the second. Thus it is better to reduce the space somewhat between the second and the third if, obviously, one wishes to maintain a proper distance.

False Distances

They are so called when the horse, by himself or his rider's prompting, must shorten or lengthen his stride or strides within the combination in order to be able to jump the second or third obstacle. This problem, however, must be at least partially solved when approaching the first.

For a short double, jump the first obstacle with a short strike-off, thereby achieving a close landing and a shortening of the stride or strides within.

For a long double, reverse the process, seeking a long strike-off and a lengthening of stride or strides within.

For a treble the problem is posed and solved in the same way; but the course architect has a great variety of combinations to choose from: the distance between the first and second fence may be right, but that between the second and third long or short, or, the other way around, the first distance may be short or long, the second right. He also may place a short distance between the first and second, a long between the second and third, or the other way around. The latter set-up, by the way, is really tough. Where the problem of both long and short distances is posed within the same combination, going "right" on the second keeps us from having to modify much on the first and third.

For two obstacles to be considered a double, the distance between them must not exceed 12 m. (39 ft. 4½ ins.), yet not fall short of 4 m. (13 ft. 1½ ins.). In the latter case the horse makes a standing jump, striking off just where he lands, without taking a stride.

Water Jumps and Brooks

At the core of our difficulties here is the fact that they are too seldom seen on horse show grounds. Lack of habit on the part of the rider, lack of training on the part of the horse. And yet they do not require too great an effort of the horse, the average jump being about 15 ft. at most. Wider they are rarely found, the Olympic being 5 m. (16 ft. 5 ins.); the only difficulty really is to make the horse get as close as possible, therefore diminishing contact and permitting the neck to stretch. I look upon water jumps and brooks the way I do upon a triple bar; and the only trouble I have found there has been in getting the horse to jump at all, a problem of a different kind that we shall deal with where it belongs, in the section on Schooling.

Banks

There is such a variety that it is hard to pinpoint a manner of negotiating them. If the horse is well acquainted with this sort of obstacle and you thus need not worry about refusals, you had best lead him there in good balance, leaving him his head for best use of his neck, then let him manage. The bank is a natural and massive obstacle he respects. It is above all a question of his keenness and address; the best you can do is follow and encumber him as little as possible, while giving him the required impulsion and speed.

Banks are roughly of three types:

1. Somewhat sloping with space at the top for the horse to take one or two strides, then jump down the other, open-edged, side of the bank. When taken in this direction it is downward, the other way around it is upward and then to be taken the way we would a straight fence, though not standing off.

2. Very sloping with a more or less rounded top and redescending more or less steeply. Depending on the slope and height of the exit, it may be all the way from impressive to truly difficult. Sometimes the horse is practically seated and cannot help sliding.

3. Usually preceded and followed by a ditch, it is composed of two almost vertical planes, the top rounded without sufficient surface for the horse to set down his four feet at once, so that he must at the end of the take-off be able to place his forefeet on the top, then draw his hind feet practically to the same spot vacated by the forefeet which just then start to descend. This kind is, of course, the hardest bank to jump, requiring an adroit and agile horse, precision of the rider's aids and, above all, great lightness of body and hands.

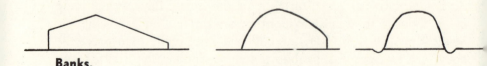

Banks.

CHAPTER NINE

Analysis of a Course

The analysis of a course begins at home, with the examination of the following points:

Are we objective in the knowledge of our mount? Not even the best horse is in top shape 365 days a year. This we should remember in making our entries. Having him do less rather than more than he can do, at least we do not run the risk of damaging him in spirit, if not body, and then losing perhaps an entire season giving back what we have taken from him in a couple of rounds. As far as possible, we should know ahead of time what is awaiting both of us, whether the grounds have natural obstacles and of what nature. There is scant salvation in inspecting inappropriate banks and water jumps the day of the event. Also, quite obviously, we should be well aware of the conditions of the particular class we are entering.

This dealt with, we have on our hands the ultimate preparation of the horse for the specific class or classes chosen. If in good training, he may be expected, three days before the event, to round a course of height and width conditions similar to those of the event, though it is strongly advised to keep the number of jumps to seven or eight. The remaining two days will see only normal work at the three gaits. It cannot do harm to wrap up those last sessions with a couple of jumps over a 3 to 4 ft. fence, provided this is all and reward is forthcoming thereafter; that is, a return to the stables and not another working session to try to improve his form. If this jump is to be registered by him as a relaxation, almost a reward, after conscientious work, the fence in question must be quite a bit lower than what he can actually manage. Think of it in terms of an elementary school teacher who, having held the children's sustained attention, wraps up the class with a good joke before sending them out for recess.

If we have studied the course on paper before pacing it off, we will then only have to check what we have memorized. The true value of course inspection lies in the study of each fence in relation to the one before and after. There also may be variations in ground level, especially important when we must, for example, jump a straight fence on an ascent, no matter how slight. The ground conditions are equally important for landings and turns. Consider the place of the sun. Will we have it smack in our eyes in just a moment? Will it be reflected in the water jump, very likely to cause trouble? Such things may be somewhat remedied by taking those obstacles on the oblique.

Then there are the distances not only within the combinations but between separate obstacles which are not very far apart. It has been found that where two fences are less than 40 yards apart, the second comes up right for the average horse if the distance between them is a multiple of 10 ft. (50 ft., 60 ft., 70 ft.), this being all the more interesting when the obstacle just before a combination is within such limits. It may help us negotiate the double or treble. Just as interesting is the distance between a fence and a turn. Another helpful thing to know is the solidity of an obstacle. Some poles are barely poised and a whiff can tumble them. There you had better take a most careful jump. Others are nice and solid and, if not treated too familiarly, a light touch may be risked if time is gained by standing off a bit; for a pole touched lightly with the forelegs is very liable to fall, while one touched not too strongly with the hind legs during the descent has a good chance of holding up. Watch and see during the next two or three shows you attend as a spectator.

The chronometer, whenever it counts, usually makes the difference between the first and second place. My own instructor used to say, "for a fast round start by not losing time." It is quite fantastic to see a rider make a fast round look as if he were going slowly and another give the opposite impression because he canters sharply, being in reality much slower. The latter's turns are necessarily wider and he must slow down rather far from the jump to

reorganize his horse, while the former is free to lengthen the ultimate strides without fear of being unable to turn short just after
it. None of these means are beyond a somewhat orderly rider with
a bit of brains, chiefly when the event takes place outdoors where
the grounds are much larger than the course itself and the fences
widely spaced.

On the other hand, speed may be increased by saving time
through an oblique jump or a turn during it. Both time-saving
devices cannot be improvised and require careful preparation,
address and keenness of the horse and precision of aids in the rider.
I hardly need explain how to jump obliquely; all is in knowing the
possibilities of our horse and not asking him for something he
cannot give. *Turning in the air* requires a very good seat and just
as fine a steadiness. The rider makes his inside hand and leg act as
soon as the horse leaves the ground. Wanting to turn left, he yields
with the right hand while the left executes a direct rein of opposition
and the left leg acts backward to push the haunches to the right,
leaning forward and to the left. Commensurately with his degree
of schooling the horse pivots more or less on his forelegs when they
touch down and is ready to canter in the new direction when the
hind legs touch down.

Of course, there also is the manner of starting the round. Not
to waste time, the starting line should be crossed at the speed of
the course, not difficult to do but not generally thought of. One
can even gain a bit if the first obstacle is practically harmless. We
may before the starting line set a pace swifter than that of the
course and check only after the first obstacle, thus slipping one
tenth of a second into our pocket right away. The first obstacle
is usually parallel to the starting line, so that it is best to arrive
perpendicularly to it. If, however, the first is on the right or left,
we had better cross the line obliquely to bear down on it as straight
as possible. Another tenth of a second easily saved.

When riding several horses in the same class, we make our
first round with the lesser prospect, a sort of dress rehearsal; and
if one is about as good as the other and time counts, we may take
those few chances on the first round we should hate to take on the
last. At all events, if we are aiming for first place, we ought to
know the performances preceding ours, how many have finished
their rounds by then and how many are still to come. It is the job
of team captain, coach or, if we are on our own, a friend to know

where most faults are being committed and to give us a quick briefing on the two or three best rounds so far.

It depends on the nature of our horse whether we have set him on his legs long or shortly before the performance, and this with a longer or shorter work-out. What matters is to put him in his very best moral and physical condition for the work expected. This setting him on his legs is a must for one and every horse; only the manner varies.

This, then is what you can draw from a course analysis and why inspection on foot before rounding it is necessary, not only to be permitted but encouraged, I repeat. Coaches and instructors should explain its function and how we can learn, with the help of experience, to make use of it, thereby teaching us to ride with our heads. Shows are a waste, at least from the standpoint of equitation, unless we learn something from each finished round. To deprive competitors of inspecting the course is not only unfair, particularly to the first poor guinea pigs to pass, but also handicaps the progress of novices who should be given guidance and a chance to learn how to evaluate the difficulties they must solve. No better place to teach them straight reasoning than where practice, so promptly following theorizing, cannot fail to confirm or rebut on the spot.

CHAPTER TEN

The Goal Attained

The education of the rider over the fences may be summed up as follows:

1. Suitable exercises develop gymnastically good seat, steadiness and balance before and during the jump.

2. When this purely material point is reached, he trains over simple courses with an experienced horse. During this period he is still looked upon as no more than "the necessary evil" in the horse-and-rider association and must perfect his equestrian feel to where he follows, and ceases to encumber, his horse, merely giving the necessary impulsion and direction.

3. At a certain distance from the obstacle the necessary intervention is practiced which serves to put the horse in proper balance and gives him the impulsion and speed needed for jumping the fence where he is being led.

4. With some talent and experience the rider now can place the strike-off just where he deems it best for his horse and thus modify the trajectory of the jump. This choice of strike-off can be valid only if during the third phase he has learned to lead the horse there in proper balance, at the right speed and with the necessary impulsion.

Intervening thus in the horse's way of jumping, the rider cannot afford mistakes of choice or aids, and his horse must be well-schooled enough to understand these actions.

Their dialogue is of a wider range and far more subtle, both having reached this refinement through the work of many months.

Difficult and demanding of precision as it is, this kind of riding is really the *haute-école* of jumping, taking talent plus experience—that is, the absolute control of the impulsion, balance and speed making a good jump. Only when all this is present can a proper choice of the take-off spot change a good into an excellent jump.

Part II

The Education of the Horse

Neck and forelegs in a perfect gesture.

CHAPTER ELEVEN

Training and Schooling: Meaning and Technique

The Trainer

The horse we want to school over the fences is taken on when still a colt and his early education is just about the same as that of a dressage horse. There is the same imperative of winning their trust, respect and thus obedience. Their bodies must be developed and their capacities increased through healthy feed, good hygiene and intelligent exercise; a timid and fragile colt is to be turned into a horse sound in body and mind.

Thus the trainer's chief preoccupation is to graduate his demands so as not morally and physically to blemish him and jeopardize his future training. This graduation is one of the greatest difficulties, if not indeed the foremost, in training a young horse. Though there are, of course, general guidelines by which we should abide if we do not want to go wrong, there are no type-progressions to be blindly applied regardless of the horse's reactions. So the trainer must rely on his sense of observation in understanding his pupil and establishing the proper progression. This sense of observation obviously can function only if combined with experience and an indispensable knowledge of the principles of classical equitation.

Before he even starts he must establish his goal and determine by which means he will attain it. Once he applies them in his work, each session in itself should have a well-defined aim and he should abstain from any demand not corresponding to a *precise* idea of what he expects of his horse or out of context with the object of the lesson.

Whatever our particular aim, there is one, general but essential because it comprehends all of equitation, toward which all and any training must be oriented, to have a horse CALM, FORWARD AND STRAIGHT, and to be achieved in just this order; because if the latter two are not necessarily acquired *fully* in each and any kind of training, the former must be complete. In such quiet composure only may we hope to obtain the useful impulsion we need and which, without calm, would grow into a source of almost insurmountable difficulties.

Maybe all this needs clarification. Anyone can, of course, make use of his sense of observation; but is it acute and pertinent? And if so, does he draw the right conclusions therefrom? This requires not only talent and experience, but the ability to take his own measure as concerns this sense of observation, talent and experience.

Whatever our limitations, we should beware of imitating a more accomplished trainer we admire without an underlying understanding of the *why* and *how*. In equitation, understanding is FEELING. But in training, to feel not only means to realize when one hock is stiffer than the other but to be aware of what is going on in the colt's head, his joys and fears and weariness, in sum, his character. Since here is the true key to success in elementary training, it takes a good deal of experience with young horses before one may venture to train a colt with any real hope of success. Never during all the elementary training must he lose his good spirits or return to the stables sad because disheartened or ground down with fatigue; on the contrary, he should always be physically relaxed, not broken, and morally intact. Though morale never loses its importance, I insist on it particularly during the training period, because those first few are the most fragile, one might say brittle, months. If this first education has been successful, the dangers lessen by and by. The horse's morale has been tempered, the trainer's tact has become refined, both will be better acquainted. If in work and lessons the master does not abuse his pupil, the latter—like a child not physically or mentally overtaxed in school—will return day after day gaily and without apprehension, sure of timely rewards for efforts not beyond his possibilities. I know of nothing as pathetic as a sad child, except perhaps a sad colt; of nothing more charming than the sight of either, gay and trusting; of nothing more odious than an unmannerly creature, be it colt or child. Such an education requires calm, gentleness, patience and firmness.

Though just at first we should be content with little, still each lesson should mark a measure of progress, however slight. Not to require this would be a sterile patience. One of the French masters remarked that we should rather say *give a proof* than *make a show* of patience, since patience in itself has nothing positive.

Yet we only can expect such daily progress if we know not only our final purpose but that of each lesson: whatever we wish to teach or improve in relation to the previous one. "Well, certainly," you will say. Yet in practice it is far from so. Col. Cavaillé (a remarkable teacher, as well as an excellent horseman and team captain) made this quite clear during an instructors' course: "Let a number of, obviously advanced, riders work on their own for ten minutes and then pick out two or three at random with a query as to the purport of their doing, and three-fourths of the time you fail to receive a satisfactory reply." Only too true, since some in my own study group with him were caught *in flagranti*. When later I occasionally asked the same question I seldom got a good reply. What kind of progress can you expect of your horse if you yourself do not exactly know what you want to obtain? Training and Schooling is like a stairway. The final aim is the top, but you may choose among a number of ramps, all leading to the same successive landings. The successive aims are like such landings which must be attained in order to reach the very top or final goal. The individual steps stand for the progress of each individual day. The pursuit of a horse calm, forward and straight is a long and arduous climb.

Once more a little clarification is in order.

CALM: The need for a calm horse seems quite obvious. It is unthinkable to ask even the simplest movement of a horse engaged in more or less overt revolt. There is no sense in going any farther as long as absolute calm has not been secured, for one can no more be a little calm than one can be a little sane. Incomplete, it is simply inexistent. Moreover, it is easier to obtain than to preserve, standing and falling with the rider's wisdom in graduating his exigencies, not to exasperate his horse. CALM IS THE SETTING FOR THE INSTRUCTION OF A TRUSTING HORSE.

FORWARD: The forward movement must be pursued and preserved throughout Training and Schooling and subsequently will remain the rider's principal concern. The horse must advance keenly at the first prompting of his master's legs, and this in any type of equitation whatsoever, though in *haute-école* this form ceases to suffice, another, superior kind taking its place, made possible only through the suppling of the joints. This suppleness makes them flexible enough for the airs of *haute-école*, and here the forward movement is expressed through their constant, total play, extended gait or not, because the action gains in height whatever it may lose in extension. Its illustration *par excellence* is the piaffer.

STRAIGHT: The horse is straight when, on a straight line, it does not deviate from it. This must be achieved regardless of the horse's final destination, the propulsive forces pushing the horse in his entirety toward the given direction. This elementary requirement suffices in ordinary equitation, not in *haute-école* where straightness must be perfect from head to croup, the hind legs following the same track as the forelegs. Without absolute rectitude of haunches and shoulders the movements could not be correct.

Such perfection of the horse's forward movement and rectitude not being part of stadium jumping, they need not, as I said, reach such a point; but it is indispensable to obtain easily and with alacrity the forward movement, while keeping the horse tautly oriented in a given direction.

Throughout training we have a set of traditional principles to guide us and to respect:

—Never undertake any work unless quite clear in your mind what you want to obtain.

—Go from the known to the unknown, from the simple to the complex.

—Apply like aids to obtain like effects.

—Position precedes action.

—Never demand anything of a horse still vibrating under the impression of a previous demand.

—Never combat two resistances at once.

—Recognize the moment when the horse has understood, so as to yield in time.

—Ask for whatever is new at the end of your work.

—Demand slight progress at each lesson, but leave well enough alone.

—Let the horse stretch his limbs, oblige him to do so, after executing slow or collected movements, because this kind of work may provoke general contraction or loss of impulsion.

The Horse

Once you decide to buy a horse, consider the following points:
—origins
—conformation
—gaits
—form over the fences (at liberty)
—the result of a veterinary check-up

Let us assume our horse is four years old or almost, has never been ridden and thus cannot be tried under the saddle. There is no guarantee, despite the counsel of expert and veterinarian, what the future will bring; but if the check-up is positive we may be reasonably sure of our buy.

The origins give us an idea, if not a very definite one, of the horse's character and physical possibilities.

Obviously conformation is important. The first thing to look for is harmony, although there is a point in mass and height, because our sometimes faulty balance will thus have less repercussions and the obstacles present less of a challenge. But do not sacrifice high breeding to such considerations. No beauty could make up for its lack. Only the high-bred horse is made of steel, the others are at most of iron.

What matters most is good natural balance, assumed to be so if the line from the top of the shoulder to the point of the hip is short (about the length of a head) and if, on the contrary, the distance between the point of the shoulder and the last false rib is long compared with the top-of-shoulder-point-of-hip line. If the difference between them is really great and the first line is truly short, you may be sure of fine withers and shoulders.

The chest must be only slightly less high (1 to 3 or 4 ins.) than half the horse.*

Good conformation of the croup is of the essence. The necessary energy to pass an obstacle comes from the release of the hind legs. The ilium must be broad (taken at the point of the hip), its inside angle conspicuous, standing out from the lumbar vertebrae. The croup itself should not slope too much.

Beware of badly-hung-on necks.

---

* This measure is valid only with a fully grown animal, and full growth varies with the different breeds, Thoroughbreds being the most precocious.

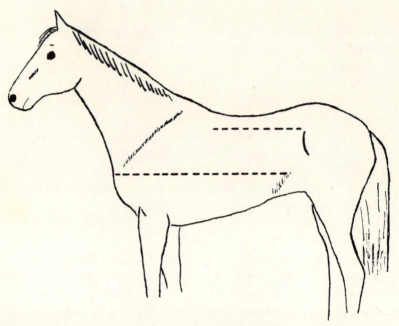

Relative lengths of back and scapulo-femural lines.

Ewe-neck.

Regular formation of the legs at the halt and at all three (easy and fluent) gaits.

When you make your prospect jump, put the poles on the ground to begin with, let him look and sniff at them and pass them three or four times at a walk and trot. Raise them to 1½ ft. with a guard rail. If he stops do not hustle him but make him jump, then go up to 2 ft. What you want to see is how, coming on at a trot, he uses his neck, if he raises his shoulders, if he tucks in his forelegs, if he uses a proper bascule movement.

If all this, and the veterinary check-up, turns out satisfactorily, you probably have a nice jumper. I am not discussing all points of the horse, though they may be relevant to choice. Enough books, including my own *Equitation: Learning and Teaching*, have spoken of them.

Since we have chosen a young, totally ignorant horse, barely four years old, we need two years to make a show horse of him. This time includes, of course, his physical preconditioning and does not preclude further schooling for improvement after the horse is already in action. Most certainly, this period may be shortened, but I advise against it and prefer to give you an example of classical Training and Schooling.

We may, of course, buy a horse that has already been ridden, raced or jumped; but we cannot deal with every possibility. We would, anyway, have to work toward the same successive aims, and if some would be attained more quickly with such a horse than could be in the progression below, others would, on the contrary, take longer because he would have to unlearn a number of things. In the last analysis, it is easier to train well than to retrain, to "cut from new cloth" than to make alterations.

Our aim is to develop physical capabilities to the high point where the horse becomes an "athlete" and at the same time obtain submission to the aids, moral properties adding effectiveness to the physical, the former obtained through *the lessons*, the latter developed through *the work*. This is attained, as we know, in two stages— *Training* and *Schooling*—which, combined, add up to *Dressage*.*

---

* *Dressage*, "the systematic training of a horse in obedience and deportment" (Webster's International, 1964), is the entire process of training, and a *dressage test* is just exactly what it says: a test of the accomplishments of the horse's dressage.

D

Training and Schooling

THE TRAINING lasts about ten to twelve months, including two periods:

A. Acclimatization of the young horse to his new life.

B. Training proper.

Period A lasts about three weeks, purporting only to accustom the horse physically and morally to his new existence.

Period B develops the physique through daily *lessons* and *work* and lays the groundwork, solid within its simplicity, whereupon the Schooling of the following year will be built. It is during this first year that the trainer must win and never lose his pupil's trust.

The Work is given only once a day, addressing itself to the physique: muscling; development of wind; canter; execution of known movements. For hygiene's sake we do it, whenever possible, outdoors.

The Lessons may take place once or several times a day, must be short and have a definite aim. Their purpose is to teach the new and to perfect the familiar.

Such training should give us a horse

—perfectly sound and unblemished

—obedient on the longe at all three gaits on both hands

—calm when working at liberty

—forward at the action of both legs

—yielding to the action of the single leg by shifting his haunches

—tightening his reins and yielding to hand action

—obedient and calm at the three gaits in the ring and outside

—knowing the opening, neck and direct opposition reins

—keenly jumping small obstacles.

Remember that a well-trained horse is more than half schooled.

THE SCHOOLING continues the work and the lessons, perfecting the results obtained in Training. The horse now becomes more sensitive to the aids, yields with lightness to the indications of hands and legs; the rider is able to shift balance, speed up or slow down gaits without depriving them of keenness and ease, in the indoor and outdoor ring, across country or on an obstacle course. The horse's knowledge of curb and spur makes communication now more wide-ranging and more finely shaded. The introduction to *ramener* and engagement of the hind legs will gradually lead to collection. Balanced, with a supple top line, light, used to cantering and turning on the outside lead and changing lead at the master's prompting, the horse has become easy and pleasant to ride. They are the same qualities as required for a dressage horse, and, if we develop them in logical sequence and add to this simultaneous exercises over the fences, our colt will turn not only into a pleasant ride, but an efficient jumper. The difference between a trained and a schooled horse is that one is *serviceable,* the other *agreeable.*

CHAPTER TWELVE

Acclimatization

On arrival at his new home the young horse is granted three weeks or so before the start of work, a period not only for acclimatization but for taming through acquaintance. If we have the facilities, we might isolate him from other horses to avoid the risk of contagion. This is the time TO WIN HIS CONFIDENCE, TO CARE FOR HIS PHYSIQUE AND GET HIM USED TO HIS NEW FEED.

To win his confidence means, we know, to learn to understand him and to teach him to understand us, best accomplished by daily, oft repeated contact. If our visits do not always coincide with work but rather more pleasant occasions, our voice becoming familiar, our tone not splitting his ears, we will soon have his trust. The voice is too precious an aid to be wasted, particularly since the horse, by his strongly developed hearing, is affected by the subtlest intonations. Shouting in the stables and during work is a taboo extending, of course, to the grooms. Hearing a stableman speak to his horse while mucking out or grooming gives us a pretty good idea of his worth. I have never yet met a good one in the habit of shouting. While this is not to say that a groom who does not shout is necessarily good, the one who does most certainly is not. A horse should be spoken to calmly, gently, though naturally and with self-assurance.

The feed must be abundant and varied. Its basis is hay. High-grade hay has all that is required for a horse doing minimum work. The added ration of oats, being exciting, is increased only gradually. Its quantity must depend on breed, size and work load. Though good and useful pellets are on the market, with a horse just in from pasture it is wiser to make the first transition through hay, adding the blends by and by. We should be watching the droppings for worms or signs of ill digested food. A clean bucket of water at stable temperature is a permanent fixture in the box, refilled as often as required.

Let us remind ourselves that physiological "upkeep and, the more so, restoration are limited by the individual's nutritive potential, while organic expenditures easily exceed this limit, and then the animal is sacrificed to the greed or ignorance of man." (Jacoulet & Chomel)

Our horse is groomed every day. Too many consider this as just a cleansing process, forgetting its effect as a massage. Because of these two very distinct purposes no technique, however efficient, can cut down grooming to five or ten minutes. The horse is cleaned for the pores to breathe freely and massaged to relax the muscles and activate the circulation. The legs are hosed down after work, wiped with a clean, dry rag in winter, but not rubbed, to avoid chapping at the pastern. The feet are cleaned while grooming and once more after work, kept in condition with grease on the walls and undersides. At least once a month the farrier pares and fits them with light shoes. Heavy ones are needlessly tiring for the tendons. In winter we use blankets, in summer simply sheets.

Here we shall mention once and for all the precautions taken in exercise, valid not only during acclimatization but throughout Training and Schooling. Though quite distinct as to their aims, the three periods are closely related in their practice and must be linked by smooth transitions. It is up to the trainer to establish this steady, fluent, unbroken progression.

I cannot over-emphasize the importance of calm during lessons and work, without a hint of impatience or nervousness. It is better to abstain than to give a bad lesson; the horse has an excellent memory and therefore should not be made to register and store any but the best impressions.

Physically, we must take any and all precautions to prevent blemishes and accidents. It is easier to prevent than cure a splint. We thus use boots for lessons and work, the more important in the first year while horses are awkward in their gaits and their bones fragile. With improvement of the way of going we shall no longer need them for the work. Always using boots, I have noticed on their insides traces of scraping by the opposite foot. However light such blows, they had better be sustained by the boot than by the

leg. For jumping lessons kneecaps are particularly important, because a big knee is not only hard to heal but liable to recur at the
slightest shock.

During these first few weeks the daily *work* is really just a physical education session, whenever possible a simple outing, at a walk
and a slow trot, in summer preferably in the morning, in winter in
the early afternoon.

The first sessions in the ring have no other purpose than to set
the colt on his legs where he is calm and his attention is more easily
caught and retained than outdoors. They last but twenty or twenty-
five minutes. If our ring is large we fence it off so as to have our
pupil within easy reach; and, particularly the first time, we grant
him a few minutes for orientation before sending him onto the
track for ten minutes' trotting on each hand.

Unless our outside ring is well fenced-in and of about the same
size as the *manège* (70 to 80 ft. x 45 ft.), we use the longe there for
walk and trot on a wide circle on both hands. If gentle, we soon let
him occasionally walk, and sometimes slowly trot, in hand.

Right from the start we should hold a training whip, tip to the
ground, and send the horse onto the track with it, always tip down,
always with a slow gesture. If we use it discreetly and do not wave
it around, it will not cause him any worry.

We will get to where we obtain a calm walk and trot and the
halt by the voice. We carry carrots for frequent reward and leave
the halter on at first, more easily to retrieve him at the end of the
session; but after a few days the carrot alone should be enough to
make him follow us to the exit. He will soon understand, and to us
it will be immensely gratifying and amusing to have him thus tag
after us even when we do not head straight for the exit.

The training in the stables, naturally, goes on quite simultaneously with whatever we are doing outside and in the rings. The
horse has become accustomed to his daily care, having his feet
lifted, shifting his haunches to left and right when told, "turn," to
being lightly girthed by the roller of the stable blanket. If all this
has been managed as gently in the stables as in the rings and outside, our colt will now be nicely "tamed," as evidenced by a good
appetite, a shiny coat, vivacious but not restless eyes, calm but not
sad, gay but not turbulent. Throughout Training and Schooling we
must be keenly aware of what occurs in the stables and take it into
account in determining the progression; the stables and the *manège*
go hand in hand and greatly affect one another.

CHAPTER THIRTEEN

Early Training with Longe and Chambon

Longe Work

This work will receive scant space here, since we want little more than calm and submission at the three gaits on both hands. Nevertheless, we may need it later and had better acquaint our colt with elementary training on it which, besides, is useful for exercising when he cannot be ridden and circumstances do not permit work at liberty. Moreover, it lays the groundwork for a simple but precise language between pupil and master and teaches the horse obedience to the voice. It constitutes a real difficulty for the beginning trainer, however, and so we shall do without it whenever possible, particularly at the canter.

If we have a hot horse we exercise him at liberty, then carefully adjust the cavesson, not too loose, lest it act too severely, nor so tight or low as to impede respiration. Be sure the cheek straps (chiefly the outer) do not touch the eyes when the longe tightens. It might be wise to have an aid within earshot, but we give the lesson proper alone. If our horse is mischievous enough to make us fear, in the beginning, that he might reverse the rôles and put *us* on the longe, we fence off as much of the riding hall as we need for our circle. This way he will not be tempted to drag us all over. Above all, there must be *calm*, the cardinal condition in training, particularly in the beginning.

We are now standing at the near side of the horse and have just attached the longe to the cavesson, holding the line at about two feet from him, the remainder folded in figure eights in our left hand which also holds the longing whip, *point down and back*. In this manner we make him describe two or three rather large circles. If he leaps forward, we calm him with our voice and shake the longe with the right hand (not too harshly, don't make him afraid to advance). If on the contrary, he is not advancing freely, we fall back a step or two and cluck to him.

As soon as calm forward movement has been obtained, we let the longe slip a little, continuing to walk with him, at a somewhat greater distance, describing a smaller circle concentric to his. Little by little we should be able to put twelve to fifteen feet between him and ourselves. We keep on walking on a small circle, moving toward his quarters to speed him up, toward his forehand to slow him down. At this point we shift the longing whip to the right hand, holding it as before, effecting the change-over behind our back so as not to frighten our pupil.

We shall not be too demanding of work and submission during these first lessons: their main object is to get the horse used to the longe, the whip, his trainer—in other words, his work.

After a few turns at a walk, we ask him to TROT, by clucking discreetly while showing him the tip of the whip. If he has never been beaten and we are doing this right, he has no more reason to be afraid of the whip than of our hand. We try to obtain a trot which, if not academically smooth, at least is joltless and calm. We encourage him by voice: "Good, go-od . . . fi-i-ine," dragging out the syllables to soothe him. To bring him back to a walk, we shorten the longe progressively and walk toward him, saying, "a-t a w-a-l-k." Later we shall be able to stay where we are, but we want to teach him to stay on his circle, even at the halt, and so we would not want to begin by teaching him to leave it. We must impress upon him the respect for the circle as we did, in the work at liberty, the respect for the track.

To bring him down to a walk, we will have shortened the longe to about three feet. With a mild vertical shake we ask him to HALT, saying, "ho." If he obeys, we pat him extensively and start over. If he repeats his performance, we reward and take him back to the stables. If he does not, we hold the longe line a couple of inches from the cavesson. With patience and firmness it should not take us long to get him to halt on the circle with us standing in a circle about three feet inside of his.

All this work must, of course, be performed on both hands.

During the following lessons we do all this work again, taking the same precautions. One day, when our pupil has been particularly calm and obedient, we will want to get him used to the touch of the whip. We pass the handle over his back, loins and croup. Holding the longe line with our left hand about a foot from the cavesson, the handle and cord of the whip in the right, sure the cord is not hanging down, we apply the whip frankly but not brusquely to the withers. If he appears worried, we calm him with our voice and then slide the whip along back and croup. The longing whip is an aid, and therefore a working utensil which he must know, respect, but not fear.

He must tauten the longe; if he tries to come toward us, we make him stay on his circle by oscillating the longe horizontally. We move it vertically when asking for a slow-down or a halt.

Horses who push their haunches too far out on a circle are rare, but many will bear in, and here the whip is useful to push the quarters back into place, so that the hind feet describe the same circle as the fore. Some will resist by "overtaking" the longe line and kicking out at us, and we must make sure that they keep the longe as taut as if they wished to move away from us and that the haunches remain where they should. For maximum efficiency, we should be the center of the circle described by our horse, whip

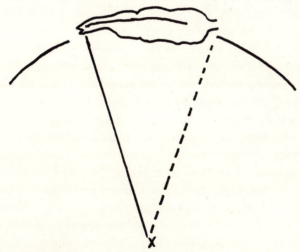

V-pattern in longeing.

and longe forming the two branches of a V, with us at the tip. Thus he is framed between longe and whip.

The Work at Liberty

While we make sparing use of longe work, the work at liberty is greatly stressed. It is begun as soon as the longe work has borne its fruit of "rudimentary" obedience. Whenever possible, we use it to introduce the horse to whatever is new: the first poles, the saddle, the snaffle, and so on. The first snaffle, by the way, is put on, reinless, in the box and left there for about an hour. The next morning we put it back a half hour before the lesson during which we leave it on. All should go smoothly if we choose quite a thick snaffle of the same width as the mouth and adjust it perfectly. All this is very important because anything new should be taught the horse without the rider's weight upon his back, thus making him more lucid to the trainer's wishes and thereby simplifying the work for both. Soon we may add the reins, entwined between mouth and breast, the throat latch between them so they will not slacken, the reins this way exerting a light tension on the snaffle.

The first time we put on the saddle we wait for the end of the lesson (which has followed the work), the horse wearing a cavesson, instead of the snaffle. We hold the longe rather short while an assistant pats his back, puts on the saddle, bare of stirrup leathers, and girths gradually, just enough to keep the saddle from turning. The colt will naturally try to buck a bit; but rather than punish him we soothe him with our voice. Once calm has been restored, we demand the halt, return to the head, shorten the longe, have the assistant girth some more and put on a surcingle to keep the flaps from beating noisily. Then we snap off the longe. He will try to rid himself of the cumbersome object, but we encourage him to trot calmly on the track. Soon he will do so and we then let him trot for a few minutes, reward him with a carrot and return him to the stables.

The following days will firmly root the acceptance of saddle and girth together with the snaffle. From time to time in the months to come we will have to use an assistant, but only when there is materially no other way. On the whole we should carry on our pupil's education by ourselves, especially as concerns the work at liberty.

Chambon

The lessons at liberty with the chambon begin immediately thereafter. This auxiliary, unlike most, is on no account a means for subjection. It acts only when necessary and yields instantly after the horse yields. Its purpose is to muscle the back, the neck and most specifically its base, giving the whole the proper direction, and promoting the engagement of the hind legs. It is an old gear, never found at fault, and its only difficulty lies in the trainer's ability to adjust it properly and to keep the horse at a free and regular trot.

We attach it to the headstall of the snaffle, take our horse to the riding hall and there make the final adjustments. We put the surcingle or saddle on his back, passing the girth through the loops of the chambon. At last we buckle the snap-hooks onto the bit. There is a good way of checking whether the chambon is well-adjusted: we should be able to attach the hooks easily, without having to lower the horse's head.

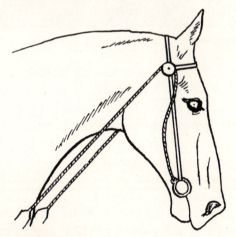

Horse fitted with chambon.

The first few times the chambon is adjusted somewhat loosely so as to avoid any resistance. Then it is tightened by and by until it is tight enough to be effective. We use an assistant at first just to snap both hooks on at once.

We want our horse to yield to the effect of the chambon by extending his neck and engaging his quarters under the mass. Some

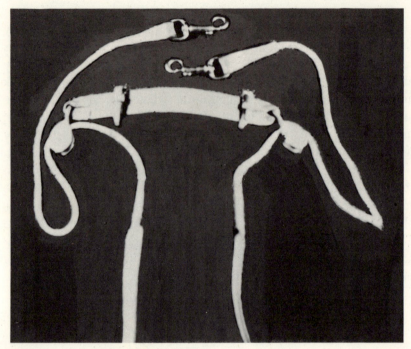

Front part of chambon.

will hollow out their backs to evade the action of the gear; this is the very opposite of what we want, so we make sure our horse is traveling under impulsion. The working gait for the chambon is the trot: a regular and calm but energetic trot.

This work with the chambon is necessary for the following reasons: the horse is not yet muscled, and this remains to be done; then those muscles must be hardened, all of them, but most particularly the neck.

Special attention is due the neck because it is an important point in the development of the horse's physical capabilities. The rider must have control over this "rudder," this "balancing pole," if he wishes to utilize it. Through it he can then control other parts of the body, most specifically the hind legs by raising the base of the neck.

The demands of our hands could later not obtain proper results without the neck responding, which it cannot unless previously hardened through muscling, then suppled into the proper orientation. Since the neck must be a flexible, tempered steel blade, not

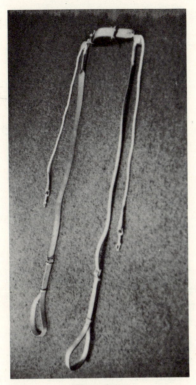

Chambon.

a piece of rubber, the tempering must precede the suppling. The orientation is of like importance because the form over the fences greatly depends on it, on its own position and that of the back during suspension, as well as on the engagement of the hind legs which, more important than ever, promotes the release at the moment of the jump and is the main factor in good balance.

All this makes the work with the chambon well worth while, the more so as it is done at liberty, simplifying the work under the saddle into which we must not hurry before our colt is physically and spiritually ready for it.

CHAPTER FOURTEEN

The First Lessons Under the Saddle

For the sake of clarity, we quite arbitrarily divide the training of the green horse into two consecutive sections: on the flat and over the fences. In practice they must remain closely linked, being as one; i.e., "the training of a jumper."

The Mounting Lesson

Given when we feel that the work on the longe and at liberty has readied our horse for the work under the saddle, it does not consist in surprising our pupil after lulling his distrust and finding ourselves on his back before he can realize what is happening. Quite on the contrary, we want him to admit the weight on his back if not with joy, at least with calm and docility. If we really want this lesson to be fruitful, we will proceed alone. No sense in using one or several assistants to hold our horse; if he is calm, we do not need them, if he is not, those people around him trying to keep him in place will most certainly not make him any calmer. Such procedures teach nothing and only engrave on his memory this mounting lesson as a frightful tussle.

After a relaxing outing in hand we have him taken to the ring saddled and bridled, where we give him a ten-minute lesson on the longe, then take it and the cavesson off, place him on the center line, lower the stirrups, regirth and adjust the reins in our left hand. While our voice reassures him, we pat the saddle, grasp the end of the stirrup leather and shake it down a few times. The

Mounting. (Photo Michel Alexis)

resultant noise and traction signal to the horse that something is about to happen on this side, our voice reassuring him that it won't be anything bad. This is one occasion to let us judge just how much of his trust we have won so far. If he moves, we set him right; that is, on the center line, his body parallel to the narrow sides. We proceed without haste, yet without hesitation, adjust our reins in the left hand and face the croup. Should he move again, we set him right again and start all over, with never a hint of impatience. We slip our left foot into the stirrup, but do not rise. If all goes well, we grasp the back of the saddle with the right hand, very close to the right flap. This way we are least liable to make the saddle turn. If he has not moved, still speaking to him soothingly, we raise ourselves lightly, without reluctance or abruptness. We keep our left toe from touching his ribs, touch down into the hollow of the saddle, neither plop nor sink into it. We put the right foot into the stirrup, its leather twisted before- hand, a small detail but likely to save us trouble. It makes the foot find the stirrup without the kind of mobility of foot and iron which is liable to worry a horse. Both stirrups thus immediately in place, we can render our seat lighter, the stirrups bearing most of the weight; and the colt, his back not overloaded, will not have to defend himself against discomfort or even pain.

Once up, we gentle him with voice and hand, waiting three or four seconds before we demand the forward movement by a click of the tongue. If we obtain it, we pat and after one or two turns around the track come back to the center, dismount, offer him a carrot and return him to the stables.

We might at first use an assistant with a training whip, who acts only on orders. If clicking of the tongue fails to elicit the forward movement, he may, standing sideways and in the back, seen by the horse, yet his action driving him forward, stress our demands with the movement of the whip, a gesture of encouragement, not punishment.

The first mounting lesson does not always go off quite so smoothly and the colt may buck, stop brusquely, whirl about, and so on. Since the trick is to stay on, and stay on passively, we had better have a stirrup leather put on like a breastplate to hold on firmly without offense to the horse's mouth. Never mind how unorthodox, this device should be used as long as necessary now, and again in jumping the first poles. Our dignity may be precious, but the horse's mouth is sacred. Furthermore, if the horseman's code says, "fault of seat venial sin, fault of hand mortal sin," during Training, chiefly its first phase, both are mortal. This makeshift breastplate lets us steer clear of both. Once in the saddle, we must stay there as long as intended. If the colt were to realize that he can rid himself of his master he would become more difficult each time, using every trick in the bag for getting rid of a cumbersome weight. We must not ever let him reach a point of rebellion where he becomes conscious of his force and our weakness. If this holds true in equitation generally, it is especially valid in Training, most particularly in its early stages.

The Forward Movement

The forward movement at the prompting of both legs will be our main preoccupation during the subsequent lessons under the saddle. Rein tension, minimal, increases very gradually and only with the horse's progress, never becoming a bother to the rider, the horse supposed to "pull his wagon," merely "poised" on the hand.

We associate the forward action of the legs with the clicking of the tongue. If it does not suffice or the horse is sluggish, we use the whip. Some are a bit absent-minded and need an occasional call to order, not punishment, applied cautiously by neat, brief contacts on the shoulder or just beyond the leg, tip down, never disturbing our seat or hand or shaking the rein in the process.

We post during these lessons, on the outside diagonal, working conscientiously on both hands. The walk, used during the rest periods, must from the first be extended to its maximum.

Combing the Reins

The chambon has accustomed our horse to extending his neck at liberty. We will start getting such extensions at a walk by combing the reins. We place the whip under our thigh and take both reins in the right hand, separated by the index finger, just as close as possible to the base of the neck. This right hand approaches our chest, letting the reins slip through the fingers, maintaining a light tension. While the right hand nears the chest, the left gets ready to act likewise, so that, as the right is finishing, the left maintains the contact by taking over, the hands relaying each other. When the horse responds by extending his neck we are careful not to let him find any resistance, yield without losing contact with the mouth in order to accompany the extension. The other hand caresses as soon as the horse starts into the extension. Realizing that the hand is light and beginning to trust it, he is not likely to refuse the forward movement. After the first sketchy extensions it is child's play to obtain them complete, the easier if our legs act properly. Once we achieve this easily at a walk, we do the same work at a trot, then at a canter.

We also do it over cavalletti and obstacles small enough for us to remain seated. Here we need considerable steadiness, hands working with precision, keeping contact with the mouth, regardless of the reactions under our seat. It is a paying exercise, one of the best in schooling over the fences, provided it is done properly. The rider being seated, his legs and seat have greater steadiness and thus his legs are more efficient.

Since these will be the horse's first mounted jumps, they will of course be rather awkward. At this minimum height (1½ to 2 ft.) there is no reason to rise, the upper body's backward motion very limited on account of the limited height of the jump. But here, and this is most important, we obtain two interesting results:

a) the horse gains confidence in our hand at the moment of the jump;

b) he is encouraged to make maximum use of his neck during the jump while orienting it properly.

The Halts

These are another of our concerns in the first lessons under the saddle. If pulling is wrong in riding, in training it simply shows that the trainer is not worthy of the name. At first we associate our voice with the action of our hands. If we have the necessary steadiness and know how to use the weight of our upper body, we should not usually meet with difficulties. We hold up our wrists and put the weight of the upper body at the end of the reins, making our hands act alternately in close succession.

The Turns

At this stage they are effected only by the OPENING REIN, because it is easily understood by the horse. Later the NECK OR COUNTER-REIN and the DIRECT REIN OF OPPOSITION may be used.

THE OPENING REIN. All is in the difference between *traction* and *attraction*. To turn left, maintaining and if possible augmenting the forward movement, we *attract* the horse's head to the left by shifting our left hand to the left and slightly forward after it has pivoted a quarter left turn to bring the nails up, the *left rein* remaining taut. The right hand first *yields* as much as necessary to permit the leftward shift of the head, then *resists* to limit the bend of the neck which must stay minimal. Hand action is limited to two quite distinct actions:

1. Setting the head of the horse in the new direction by acting with the hand on the side of the turn (left hand to turn left); the other hand yielding to permit the leftward shift of the head.

2. The hand which yielded in the beginning now resists, both

hands content to maintain the head in the new direction. ONLY THE LEGS, DRIVING THE MASS FORWARD, ARE ABLE TO ENGAGE THE HORSE in the direction already taken by neck and head.

This is the place to speak of the counter-rein and direct rein of opposition, although they cannot be taught the horse at the same time and for a while the opening rein will have to do. The counter-rein may be taught as soon as the horse yields easily to the opening rein. The direct rein of opposition, the rein *par excellence* for stadium jumping, can be taught only after the legs are able to determine a keen forward movement, the rider having his horse in front of him when in motion.

THE NECK REIN. While it is not much use with a trained horse, it is very handy during training because, contrary to popular belief, it does not detract from impulsion but prompts the horse to go forward.

This is how we will teach the neck rein to our pupil: We use an expansive opening rein to put him on a large volte, say, on the left hand. When two-thirds of it have been done, we lessen the intensity of the opening rein and use a right neck rein to take him back to the track. Do not expect too precise a figure. If he does not seem to understand, we describe two or three voltes on the same spot, using only the opening rein, very calmly, without too much insistence of the legs, caressing all the while, particularly during the last third back to the track. When we try again to finish the volte off with a neck rein, he will most certainly respond, and then we do not forget to pat him and let him walk around once or twice on long reins. Then we start over at the same place.

Here I would like to emphasize the importance of taking our time and giving our horse a chance to associate the learning of something new with a reward from his trainer. He must be taught item by item, little by little; therefore no movement should be allowed unrequested, or other than requested, by our aids. It might complicate or even jeopardize his subsequent training.

When we use our right neck rein in the example just given, reins separated, we move the right wrist from right to left and back to front, in the direction of the horse's left ear, against the growth of his hair. The intensity of this rein effect depends on the pressure exerted on the neck and the frequency of wrist movements, not rein tension or amplitude of gesture. If at first we must exaggerate the movement of the hand, accompanying it with our forearm, so that our pupil will understand and yield thereto, eventually it should be practically imperceptible. From all this it is easy to see that the neck rein, far from detracting from impulsion, adds to it. Not acting directly on the mouth, it sometimes may be very useful.

THE DIRECT REIN OF OPPOSITION. This rein acts on the horse by opposing the shoulders to the haunches. The horse yields easily to it and it facilitates tighter turns than would be possible with the first two rein effects. Moreover, it gives us control over the engagement of the hind legs when combined with the action of the outside leg (left leg for the right turn) and thereby keeps the horse in the given balance or puts him back into it if altered through excess weight on the shoulders. It cannot be taught until the neck, having been muscled, can convey its effect to the whole horse; otherwise it would affect only a neck yielding like a "rubber block" and have scant, if any, result.

The acting rein (right for the right turn) must do so backward parallel to the horse's axis, tension increased by a STRONGER CLOSING OF THE FINGERS, a TURN OF THE WRIST, NEVER BY BACKWARD TRACTION. At this early stage we should keep the active hand slightly outward. To teach the horse to yield to it easily and not to detract from impulsion, the outside hand yields and the inside hand does not act.

Example: For a right turn, the left hand yields, the right hand remains passive (neither yields, nor acts, but RESISTS). Thus the horse is turning at a yielding rather than a resistance. By and by you turn right by acting with your right hand. At all events, even later, the passive hand will always yield before the other acts. The brisker the gait, the tighter the turn, the stronger the action of the active hand, and the less pronounced the yielding of the passive hand.

I do not hold with some that one rein effect is easier to do than another. Any, to be precise, must be timely and intense enough to serve its purpose. The most important and difficult is for the hand to act with precision. If the rider is capable of this, any rein effect becomes easy.

CHAPTER FIFTEEN
Straightening the Horse

When we first ride out, at a walk and trot, we may want another, experienced horse beside ours, adjusting his gaits to those of the green horse that must be kept from jog-trotting from the very beginning. We would be hard put to break the habit later. During these rides the horse will gradually *find his new balance under our weight.*

During the whole training period we pursue two aims which at first sight may seem contradictory:

1. To muscle and tauten the young horse
2. To supple and straighten him.

There actually is no contradiction, because the suppling takes place very progressively, only after a measure of tautness has been obtained. This year of Training, after all, while suppling him to a degree, lays main stress on the muscling of the colt; and only the subsequent year of Schooling will lay full stress on the suppling, without discontinuation of the muscling process.

How is this muscling and tautening achieved? First of all by long and slow stretches outside, at walk and trot; later canter to develop wind. In the indoor or outdoor ring we work at liberty with the chambon. During the lessons under the saddle we bring the horse up to the bridle by means of the legs, pursuing maximum extension of the neck without loss of contact with the bit. Too many riders are too keen on obtaining the *ramener*, building, at this point, on sand.

THE WORK ON STRAIGHT LINES tautens the still soft young

101

horse. To keep this tautness from turning into rigidity, we require him to yield to rein action for changes of direction.

THE WORK ON CURVES OR ON THE CIRCLE UNDER IMPULSION keeps the horse taut without impairing suppleness. Let us not systematically change direction by slow-down, on the contrary; nor, as is done by many, continually request speed-ups on straight lines and change direction or negotiate corners by slow-down. For let us remember that THE HANDS INDICATE, THE LEGS OBLIGE. Equitation stands or falls with the forward movement. So we drive our pupil by excess impulsion into the new direction and do not let him evade the action of the hand by creeping behind the legs. The type of horse and the results obtained with him will determine the *work* and the shape of the *lessons*.

Horses are never straight, but usually incurved to the left. The proper exercises must rectify this as far as possible. The work on the circle is fine, but in the early stages we had better be content with exercises less liable to blemish our pupil prematurely, even if performance should fall short of expectations. Like all supplings, they require patience and perseverance, cannot be completely successful in just a few sessions. But, though perfect rectitude is rarely attained, we must never stop striving to improve it.

Two Exercises

1. We post more often on one diagonal than the other to make them absolutely symmetrical, which they are not on account of the aforementioned natural incurvation. One stride is a little longer than the other, and to arrive by and by at equal diagonals we must post more often on the left if our horse is incurved to the left. Most horses are so, and the average rider prefers to post on the right diagonal where both are more at ease. Logically we should do otherwise. Some horses are so used to being posted on the right diagonal that not only do they make it downright uncomfortable for the rider on the other, but they also put him back onto the right on their own by a false beat.

2. We allow and increase the lateral shift of the spine at a walk through alternate action of the legs, working most particularly the stiff side. At the free walk, with maximum freedom of the neck but light contact with the mouth in order to assure direction, hands accompanying the movements of the neck which should be

just as ample as possible, we carefully accentuate the lateral shift of the spine as it produces itself naturally by a pressure around which the horse seems to bend. This exercise is practiced most particularly on right curves when the horse is naturally inflected to the left. It promotes, moreover, the engagement of the hind legs.

Walking Straight

From the beginning this kind of work must receive all the necessary attention; first in the ring near the wall, then away from it, but the true work is done outside on a rectangle visually limited without restricting the horse's deviations, as would the wall of the indoor or the fence of the outdoor ring. From the very first lessons it is essential to keep carefully straight on straight lines, not to let the horse turn on his own, coming exaggeratedly inward on the curve, but to oblige him, on the contrary, to turn at the right spot and, on turning down the arena, not to let him get back onto the track before the whole turn has been finished. Withal, we will be unable to steer him properly till he learns to yield to the action of the single leg.

The Action of the Single Leg

ON FOOT: Acquainted with and fearless of the whip, the horse is placed on a rather small left circle. We hold the snaffle reins in the left hand, eight or ten inches from the mouth, standing at about mid-neck, facing the croup. A few clicks of the tongue request the walk, always on the circle, with us walking backward. We slow the walk down gradually to a minimum when, without reaching the halt, we request by repeated little taps on the thigh an outward shift of the haunches. If the walk is extremely slow, we usually achieve this at second or third try. Though the left hand holding the reins may promote the movement by drawing the horse's head very slightly to the left, we should succeed without head and neck participation. Reversing the aids, we do the same on the right hand.

IT IS IMPORTANT FOR THE INWARD HIND (THE LEFT WHEN ON A LEFT CIRCLE) TO MOVE RIGHT AND FOR-WARD, THAT IS, CROSS ITS CONGENER WHILE PASSING IN FRONT OF IT.

The shift of the inward hind must be demanded by the whip just when it starts to lift, the way we will do later in the saddle with our leg. Earlier, the prompting would be ineffective because the leg, on the ground, then carries part of the horse's weight; later, when the horse starts to touch down again, the lateral shift is very scant. The exercise must be given on both sides, with emphasis on the stiffer one.

IN THE SADDLE: Reins in one hand, we associate heel and whip action, without expecting too much just at first. By and by the heel action will suffice to obtain a shift of the haunches; later, when the way the legs are used will be far more important than the place itself, the leg will act at its normal place.

At first the other leg must remain passive; there cannot be any question of using it to regulate the movement prompted by the action of the single leg.

We accustom the horse to shifting his haunches promptly by executing broken lines, making their changes of direction by the sole action of the single leg. As the horse progresses and grows lighter to the leg, the broken lines are shortened to the point where the haunches may without the slightest resistance be swung from heel to heel.

CHAPTER SIXTEEN

The Canter

The canter has meanwhile been practiced, leaving the horse all possible scope for it in the ring or outdoors. During the first year (Training) it is chiefly done outdoors to keep it flowing and extended with all required freedom of the neck. For the moment we do not ever demand speed or endurance.

If we want to make a success of training and schooling a young horse, we must remember that muscling, tempering and strengthening is achieved chiefly by slow, sustained work. We may work up to four hours a day, if we base this on long periods of extended walk interrupted by slow, cadenced and sustained trots and canters.

Though during the second year we may canter rapidly once or twice weekly, we will not ever push the trot. Misunderstood sport, for horse and man alike, may kill rather than fortify; if we want to keep a sound horse, we must know how to graduate physical effort.

Longe Work

Earlier I said that longe work is generally delicate and that the less we do of it the more likely we are to avoid mishaps. In training it is better always to choose the simplest form; in trying to refine we easily get lost. If we are using the longe at all, then, it is in specific cases where it actually is the simplest and fastest means.

Since in this case the work on the longe is undeniably the easiest for teaching the young horse to strike off at the voice on the inside lead, we have requested the first canters on a large circle on the longe, accustoming him to cantering on the lead opposite the one he more or less emphatically prefers, as any horse will. But as soon as, at liberty in the ring, he canters on the right lead when on the right hand and on the left when on the left, we give up this longe work, which for our requirements would be a waste of time, and work at liberty where the horse is less liable to pick up blemishes. Only later, if he should not want to trot on the track for us when jumping his first poles at liberty, taking the canter for the jump, we may go back to the longe as a better means of control.

The Outside Lateral Aids

When the time comes to demand the canter under the saddle we use the outside lateral aids.

For example, on the left hand, requesting the canter on the near lead, we use the passing of a corner, tighten the right rein and act with the right leg slightly in back of its normal place, in order to aid the near lateral. The additional impulsion for the strike-off is given by a click of the tongue rather than troubling the horse by leg action requiring the shifting of one leg to place the haunches. Using inverted aids, this exercise is repeated on the right hand. Two points warrant our particular attention:

1. We should avoid traversing the horse too much. The clicking of the tongue for added impulsion is recommended just at first because it preserves the perfect steadiness of our aids (legs, hands and upper body) which only endeavor to place the horse in a position where he will canter off by himself on the lead requested. We should never try to wrest this from him; after all, he, not we, is the performer. As progress is being made, the action of the outside hand first, then of the outside leg, diminishes, the horse being kept carefully straight from shoulders to haunches.

2. Whenever the horse strikes off, let us be sure from the very first stride that the lead is correct (near lead on the left hand). The worst, however, is the disunited canter; i.e., the forelegs at the left canter, the hind legs at the right, or vice versa. Very uncomfortable for the rider, there is really no mistaking it. Though the false canter is by itself less serious than the disunited, because it is not really a defective gait, it must be repressed immediately as a disobedience, if we want the first cantering lessons under the saddle to pay off.

This work at the canter gives a measure of each rider's tact. It explains and illustrates the difference in training time required where knowledge is equal, but not tact: Requesting the canter on the near lead and receiving it on the off, the rider without tact must use his eyes to check what he actually got; with a little tact he feels it in his seat; with more he is aware that the position taken by the horse will not permit the canter on the required lead and rectifies it before making his demand; the horseman *par excellence*, highly sensitive to the contractions causing a false position, combats them from inception before the situation can arise.

The actual end of the first year has come when we are able to use the horse indoors and outdoors, when he responds easily to the elementary aids and, above all, when we have transformed a fragile, awkward colt into a sound horse in good form. Here as elsewhere, the groundwork is relatively longer and harder than the building itself, but the more solid the foundations, the more durable is the construction.

In establishing the first year's progression over the fences we are well aware that our principal purpose is CORRECT FORM and the development of physical resources. We have absolutely no intention of jeopardizing the horse's future by testing his possibilities to determine his limitations. We are not even in a hurry to begin jumping, even at liberty, or, once begun, to quickly raise the poles. We know from the start that at year's end they will not rise above 3 ft. 3 ins. to 3 ft. 9 ins. and we have about ten months to get there.

Therefore, if after the first three weeks of acclimatization—which are not part of the progression, since they neither teach nor demand anything—the horse does not seem to respond to his new existence, eats poorly and looks sad, we shall wait and not compound his bewilderment by confronting him with a set of poles. In fact, more often than not we had better wait another two or three weeks. But if he is unmistakably sound and vigorous in body and spirit, we may make this beginning practically during the first lessons. The schedule is roughly as follows:

Two or three weeks won't be too long to accustom him to obeying our voice and to familiarize him with the rudiments of training. After this period we may show him his first poles, making him jump one or two after each lesson. The best progression is the one which bases itself from lesson to lesson on the previous one.

The jumping sessions should, as all other lessons, resemble a game for the youngster, a distraction, not wearisome work. They can be useful only if given calmly, and if calm is to be preserved we need a wise progression. The crux of the matter is not to blemish the horse physically and to interest him in playing this jumping game; and so we must shun any brawl and yet obtain the performance we seek. If a fault requires sanctions, reward must follow obedience and a show of good will; and reward, easier to give well, is usually more effective than punishment. We should put ourselves into a position where we can reward often and only rarely need to punish, and this without excitement, a sort of brief "bawling out." This bawling out within an atmosphere of calm gains in effectiveness if the voice is never wasted on trifles.

I once more emphasize the importance of working alone, also during the jumping lessons at liberty. If necessary, we scale down the inside or outside ring, set up our impedimenta (poles, standards, wings) properly and have poles long enough (about 10 ft.) for obstacles with sufficient frontage and thickness (about 4 ins. in diameter). I shall not describe the classical jump standards which are well-known; but I do want to mention a less familiar kind useful for the work at liberty. It is a simple, ordinary ladder with steps which extend, however, beyond the uprights on either side. Such ladders are lighter than ordinary standards, and their feet—this is an advantage—take up less space. They are used against the wall; and the inside standard is, of course, the ordinary type. If we want our obstacle quite solid without being perfectly fixed, we set the pole or poles onto the step or steps of the ladder between the uprights, if we do not, on the outside. We do likewise for the inner standard. (See diagram.) For better channeling of the horse toward

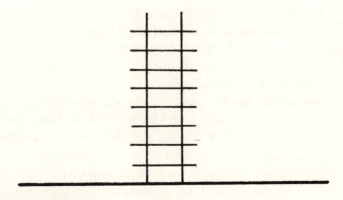

Ladder jump standard.

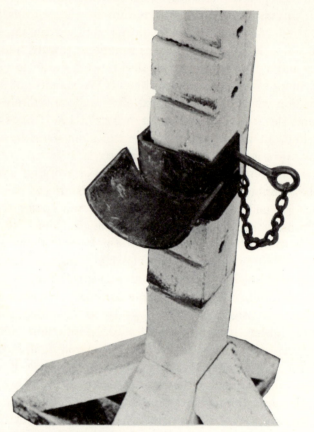

Ordinary jump standard and cup.

the obstacle we may place on each side of the standard (inner surface) a pole from summit to ground.

Before the jump, we give the colt a work-out at a walk and trot to warm him up and make him calm and attentive. Its length varies with the horse, but the calm must not be obtained by way of fatigue. Ten or fifteen minutes normally suffice.

We place a pole on the ground, either on one of the long sides or on both, letting our pupil go and have a look at them, then send him onto the track at a trot. The aim of this lesson is to have *him* trot across these poles calmly and without excitement. If he gets too wrought up, we use halter and longe, crossing the poles with him at a walk, while patting and soothing with our voice.

Then we raise the pole to 1½ ft. and place a guard rail. He jumps this set-up at the trot, as before, urged on with clicks of the tongue and the tip of the whip in the direction of the haunches. The important thing is to keep him from running out, refusing or knocking down the pole, all this work done in the greatest calm. Running out is worst of all; do not ever give it a chance. Refusal has its points because it may mean that the horse is cautious and, realizing that his approach to the jump is improper, prefers to stop. Though this kind of refusal is a good thing, approaching a 1 ft. 6 in. pole at a trot does not constitute a problem and the horse must jump it. If he commits a fault at such scant height he is probably negligent. He will, alas, remember that the obstacle dropped and from then on tend to gauge the effort necessary for "passing over" against that for "passing through." The obvious remedy for this, the fixed obstacle, however, cannot be used for the time being for fear of blemishes.

At any rate, all we want during these first lessons is to acquaint him with a few little poles without any further ado; so it should all happen just as naturally and calmly as possible. In two or three months' time we may get to where we jump a maximum of eight or ten obstacles per session twice a week; but for the moment it will only be two or three at the end of each session, JUST BEFORE RETURNING TO THE STABLES. They are no higher than 2 ft.— —little oxers wider than high. Always begin with the poles on ground level, always stay at a trot. The real training over the fences, remember, has not yet begun.

Once he is proficient in this, take away the guard rail. It helped and thereby encouraged the young horse in his very first jumps, but had to be discarded as soon as possible for teaching him to misjudge his fences which he should JUMP BY JUDGING THE SUMMIT, NOT THE FOOT.

If during these exercises he happens, as is inevitable, to knock down the pole, place it between the uprights of the ladder at the wall and in opposition to the inside standard so as to give it more stability. The next time he will either make an effort to clear, proof that he respects the obstacle and only happened to be absent-minded, or else he will knock down the pole again; but this time there is more resistance, ladder and standard come down with it, and he takes a tumble. The good horse will, after this experience, clear the next jump with inches to spare.

This does not mean that I advocate rapping. By no means! It is a little early in the text to mention this "form of schooling"; rapping is out of place in the "training period." But I had rather dispose of it here and now. Too much of it, badly done, has prompted a sharp reaction from some national federations, as well as from the F.E.I. which prohibits any form of it. If I do not preconize it, I do not proscribe it, since I feel that rightly done it may sometimes be useful. But, of course, the means is worth no more than the man, and no matter how well done, it cannot be looked upon as a schooling device. It can at best remedy to an extent the pitfalls of insufficient training or bad form over the fences due to conformation which no kind of training can completely change. Even if materially perfect, it is liable to dishearten the horse through excess. With some it works very well and so should not be condemned out of hand; but to use it excessively or without rhyme or reason, of course, is foolish; to use it with brutality is shameful. To determine absolute truth is difficult; to define it in a few words, impossible. I have schooled many a horse without ever rapping, with some I have done so for a short time. There have been some I rapped systematically, if lightly, on the eve of a show. Acceptance or rejection depend thus on why and how it is done.

Let us not confuse this with the work over fixed fences. Although the ultimate purpose is the same, a faultless jump, the applications are not. A horse dragging his forelegs because he does not tuck them in enough learns nothing over them. He only must make a disproportionate effort to clear, if his physical resources allow it, and this at an excessive expense of energies. If he lacks those energies he will become disheartened, while rapping will teach him to tuck in his legs without harming them. It is a simple call to order, less painful than striking a pole with the forelegs during a horse show. If, on the other hand, he is a "grazer," simply because he cannot be bothered with the effort, fixed obstacles are certainly much more useful than rapping. Before opting for a remedy we must know how to diagnose the ill. Rapping, at least "at home," will be going on as long as there are horses and riders. Adroit riders will profit by it, the awkward will only run into pitfalls. So while I cannot advise you one way or another, one thing is certain: never use it during training.

Always at a trot and without a guard-rail, short twice-weekly lessons will now exercise the horse over a straight fence and a low, wide oxer. What matters is that he keep calm and at a trot. The pole is progressively raised from ground level, but lowered again without reluctance if he fails to keep at a trot. The goal is a 3 ft. jump of a single pole at a trot. The goal for the spread jumps—also begun with poles at ground level, then raised and spaced—is a 3 x 3'6" jump. The progression follows the horse's progress and ability to stay at a trot.

The oxer had better not be always strictly straight. One pole may be higher on one side or higher than the other. All this is very good for the young horse. It also is a good time for showing him all kinds of checkered, motley bars and to make obstacles a little harder by placing a pole on the ground between the two bars. But go at it progressively, do not show him too many new things in one day. The familiar should remain the backdrop for the lessons. Ten jumps each session are enough, this twice a week, and do not forget the kneecaps in the tackroom.

If all goes well, we now may proceed to doubles, still always *at a trot,* the progression as follows:

a) A double consisting of two verticals at a distance of a normal stride;

b) a double consisting of a vertical and a low, wide oxer at a distance of a normal stride;

c) a double consisting of a low, wide oxer and a vertical at a distance of a normal stride.

Subsequently the distance within the last of the doubles is reduced progressively. Thus the horse, stretching to the utmost over the oxer because he gets there without *élan,* touches down unbalanced and must shift his weight back to the quarters in order to raise his shoulders and clear the straight fence. The shorter the distance between the two obstacles, the better the exercise will pay off.

This is the end of the preparatory work, taking us all the way to the threshold of the second year. To sum up, this work on foot over the fences during the first year has been given as follows:

1. During the first three weeks (acclimatization period), no obstacles.

2. During the first month or two, the jumping of two or three low poles at every lesson before the return to the stables.

3. For about four months thereafter the horse is exercised over single obstacles, beginning with straight fences, low, wide oxers, eventually alternately.

E

4. The final five months or so see the jumping of doubles as previously described.

Bear in mind that all the while the horse has only jumped at the trot, whether at liberty or under the saddle. The "lessons" at a canter do not start before the second year.

CHAPTER EIGHTEEN

Fences Under the Saddle

By the time the horse is sufficiently trained to be handy and perform satisfactorily over the fences at liberty, the training over the fences under the saddle begins. As cautious as before, we begin over poles on ground level, and this only after having answered two important questions:

1. Has he found his new balance under our weight (without, at this juncture, the artifice of alternate leg and hand action)? Hence the importance of the work outdoors on long rides while horse and rider are relaxed.

2. Is he submissive enough to our aids to be steered effectively enough not to run out or refuse?

For best results the lessons at liberty and under the saddle alternate, still always at a trot, demanding a little less under the saddle than at liberty. Above all, no pulling on the reins. With the breastplate fashioned from a stirrup leather, we keep our seat even when a jump turns out a bit eccentric, without offending the horse's mouth which should not run up against the hand at the moment he uses his neck for the jump.

With the pole against the wall to minimize steering problems, we take up under the saddle the same exercises so far performed at liberty, simplifying a bit over doubles, chiefly as concerns the width of the oxer, and eliminating as too difficult the very last where an oxer is jumped followed by a vertical.

During this entire period we must stand firm against jumping at a canter, resisting that tempting little voice that keeps whispering, "Aw, just once in a while, just to see. . . ." Nor will we get involved as yet with steering in those jumping lessons. All we want is to let our horse do his gymnastics over single obstacles or an isolated double; we are not ready to prepare for shows.

At this point the lessons on the flat, over the fences, and the daily work have come to give their joint results. If the horse's work and feed have been well handled in the past, he is equipped to take the physical effort required in obedience lessons which are always simple, clear and well within the limits of his understanding and resources. He also has acquired the correct form in jumping which spares him unnecessary effort and allows him the best possible use of his physical faculties. Again and again we must pause to analyze the status of the training on the flat. Never mind for the moment the work at a canter over the fences, our meticulous attention centers on the step by step training in order to gain the horse's submission without breaking his spirit.

Training may be considered ended when all these objectives are reached with a muscled horse knowing the simple rein effects and tolerating the rider's weight, responding to the hands with slow-downs and halts, to the legs with an advance while tautening his reins. He has been suppled on large circles or elements of curves, engaged onto them by a speed-up, not a slow-down, of the gait. No attempt at collection has been made at this stage, a concept foggily confused by many with a simple slow-down of the gait; rather a calamity in this form. We much rather seek ample movement in the gaits without precipitation of cadence. Speed-ups are never pushed to the utmost and are always brief. Improvement of the gaits is sought solely in symmetry, regularity and cadence, by frequent variations. The movements—particularly at the canter where the horse moves his neck much more than at the trot—should not be limited, the wrists should, on the contrary, accompany them, without affecting rein tension.

A review of a jumper's basic training will serve nicely as both an "epilogue" to TRAINING and a "preface" to SCHOOLING:
Work outdoors
Lessons on the flat
Lessons over the fences.
THE WORK well-handled develops physical resources, particularly muscle power, wind; that is, full functional resources. Excess may cause overtaxation, as apparent in a shrinking belly,

hollow flanks, blotchy coat, lackluster eyes, the physiognomy losing mobility and expression; it checks the development, quickly ruins constitution and opens the door to all kinds of disease. Too little work, on the other hand, is just as bad, because the horse puts on fat, becomes sluggish in its bodily functions, loses spirit and physical faculties, becomes prone to congestion and blemishes, this sluggishness accompanied by short-windedness.

THE LESSONS ON THE FLAT supple, teach recognition of the rider's signals and an easy, docile response.

THE LESSONS OVER THE FENCES give the horse his form and teach him to assume the best stance for the jump.

It is not the training and schooling over ever higher and more numerous fences which teaches the horse to jump, but the combination of lessons and work. If he has good form over 4 ft., he will have it also over 5 or even 6, provided he has the power which only well-managed work can develop.

CHAPTER NINETEEN

Bits, Bridle, Auxiliaries and Spurs

We now enter the year of Schooling. As we did with Training, we will first deal with the flat, then with the fences. This is when we initiate our pupil to a full bridle and the spurs.

Snaffles and Pelhams

So far we have used a rather thick-mouthed snaffle, sufficiently so to let the horse find his contact and, by its gentleness, to give him confidence in the rider's hand. Among the many kinds of snaffles three deserve particular attention.

THE BAUCHER SNAFFLE cannot slip sideways in the horse's mouth. Unlike with ordinary snaffles, lateral rein action cannot cause a ring to penetrate and hurt the mouth. Its cheek straps, moreover, allow for such unique precision of fit that the bit never hangs on the tongue. Depending on the thickness of its mouthpiece it may be used alone or with a curb bit.

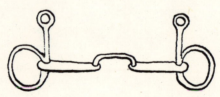

Baucher Snaffle.

THE D-SNAFFLE, the most common, may be used by itself.

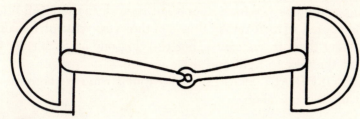

D-Snaffle.

THE FULL CHEEK BIT is a normal snaffle, also for use by it-self. The two pieces of the mouthpiece are attached to the rings which bear long and fixed cheeks preventing excessive lateral shifts.

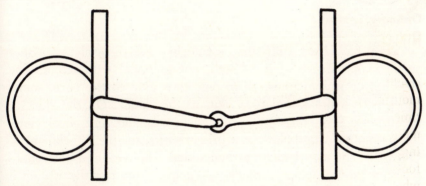

Full Cheekbit.

These three are the best for use without the curb.
THE DOUBLE MOUTH SNAFFLE BIT should also be men-

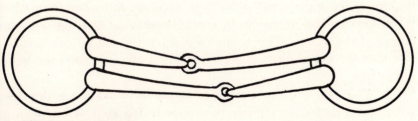

Double-Mouth Snaffle.

tioned, called DOUBLE FULL CHEEK BIT when having cheeks.
It gives good results when, a simple snaffle failing to obtain proper
relaxing at the jaw, we have reason not to wish to use a full bridle.
It is composed of two rather thin mouthpieces, without the usual
ring joining them in the center, but carrying one on each side, two
thirds of the way to right and left.

THE ORDINARY SNAFFLE with round rings is the only one
used with the chambon.

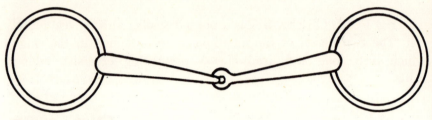

Ordinary Snaffle.

THE PELHAM BITS are a category by themselves, neither
snaffle, nor curb, related to both, not identical with either. The
mouthpiece is sometimes all in one, thus akin to the curb, sometimes with a break and then akin to the snaffle. On the sides at
mouthpiece level there are rings, as in a snaffle, and cheeks ending in another ring below, as with curb bits, for the attachment of
four reins, and a curb chain is then added. The rein used determines
whether the bit acts as a snaffle or a curb. From this description it
is quite clear that, regardless of the shape of its mouthpiece, this
bit is somehow wrong half of the time, though in some cases it
makes sense:

1. A horse with a thick tongue, narrow chin groove, or both,
will slip his tongue over the top to dodge the compression caused
by the snaffle. The height of his palate allowing, he will just leave
it there, without the novice rider even noticing. But when the palate
is too low for the tongue to fit there, he may let it hang out one
corner of the mouth. This is one case when this bit is truly useful,
provided the mouthpiece is not too thick, is all in one and the half-
moon type.

2. When a young horse tends to lie on the hand—often the case
with horses that have already been raced—this kind of bit, with a
broken mouthpiece, proves as gentle as a snaffle, yet more powerful

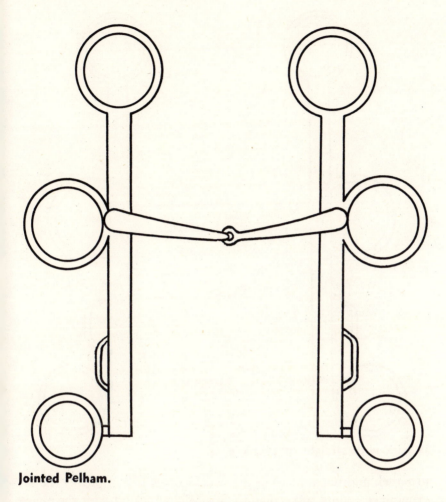

Jointed Pelham.

when the lower reins are tightened. Some riders use some butt, a BIT CONVERTER, to connect the upper and lower rings, placing thereon a single rein. Its only advantage is that they have only two, not four, reins, of purpose only with a rather awkward rider.

THE KIMBERWICK BIT is another of this category. It is above all an action bit, not to be used in Training and Schooling, chiefly useful in showing when wishing to hold back too keen a "goer," and this with but two reins.

Since they may all be looked upon as snaffles in a way and the horse carries but one mouthpiece, the fitting of all these bits is relatively simple, usually correct when, the reins being slack, the mouthpiece is in contact with the corners of the lips. Do not hesitate

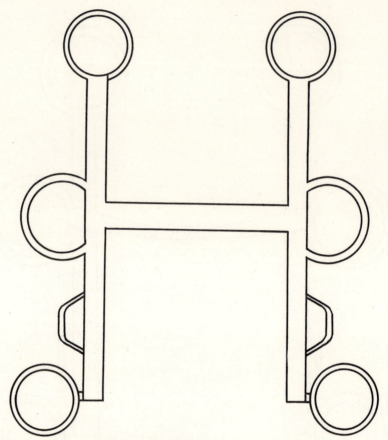

Pelham with straight mouthpiece.

to punch additional holes in the cheek-pieces if it improves the fit; experience counts, more than theory. When picking a bit for a new horse we start off with the simplest and gentlest, notwithstanding the enticements of some highly vaunted but more complicated, fancy model, because most horses respond best to what is simplest.

THE CURB BITS are not only more powerful, but their effect combines with that of the snaffle, so that we must use them in perfecting the Schooling. They may be used in competition if the horse's temperament and schooling and the quality of his rider so permit, who must cope with four reins and have a more tactful hand. Their action is stronger than the snaffle's which acts upon the corners of the lips, and this directly. The curb, on the other hand, is a *lever* and therefore transmits, multiplied, the force exercised at the end of the longer of its cheeks, with the curb chain,

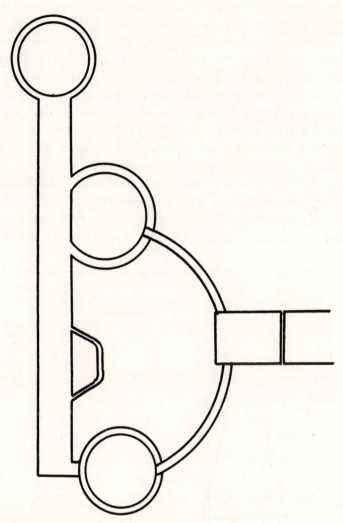

Bit converter.

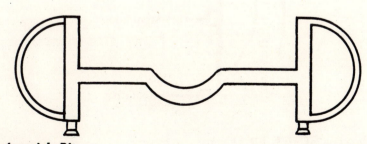

Kimberwick Bit.

an integral part of it, the point of support. The power of a curb bit is in direct proportion to the difference in length of its upper and lower cheeks—this, obviously, when the curb chain (point of support) is attached to the holes at the ends of the upper cheeks. The curb bit acts on the bars, though it lies on the tongue while the reins are slack. If, as often is believed, it acted on a tongue painfully crushed between bars and mouthpiece, we would inevitably be heading for disorder. When the chin groove (on the inside of the mouth) is rather deep and the tongue has plenty of room there, any mouthpiece will do; but rare is the lucky horse who has it, and so we had better choose a bit with an arched, not a straight, mouthpiece. Sometimes even this arch is insufficient and we must carefully pick a port-mouthed bit where the tongue finds room without a squeeze between the canal of the chin groove and the mouthpiece of the bit.

The length of the upper cheeks is important, since the curb

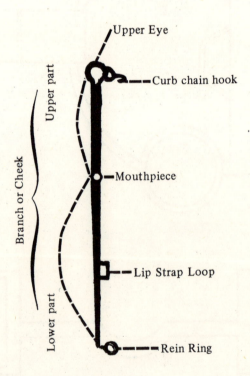

Profile view of curb bit cheek.

chain hooks are attached to the holes at their ends. If these hooks are too high the curb chain does not stay in place but rides up when the bit swings, rubbing strongly against the lower jaw. Three quarters of all injuries occasioned by the curb chain are due to this, which does not happen when the hooks are well-placed and the bit is adapted to the anatomy of the horse's mouth.

The Adjusting of a Full Bridle

Since the curb bit cannot be raised or lowered, or at most by a minimal fraction of an inch, and the snaffle must find its place between it and the corners of the lips, the determining factor in the fit of the bridle is, obviously, the curb. If lower, the snaffle passes more or less under or over the curb, warping the play of both bits. So if the corners of the lips are set rather high the snaffle is easily fitted between them and the curb; but if set low we might just have to accept the snaffle's slight lifting of the corners of the lips, the lesser evil, preferable to placing it lower, at curb level. The bridoon must be thin, take up minimum space; the width of both bits must be proportionate to the width of the mouth. The snaffle must be wide enough for its mouthpiece to form a straight line, the ends sticking out sufficiently (about 2mm.) for the snaffle rings not to touch the corners of the lips. The curb must be measured very precisely against the width of the mouth at the exact spot of its passing,

Horse fitted with Full Bridle.

and thus must be a little less wide than the snaffle, 1 mm. of play on each side between the tops of the upper cheeks. The upper jaw may actually be broader on the outside than the lower; thus the upper cheeks must be sufficiently spaced to swing freely back to front without rubbing against the sides of the upper jaw. I would recommend a lip-strap on the curb bit from the first day on. Often the horse begins by playing with the branches, taking them between his lips, but soon this game turns into a tic and subsequently a defense. Here, as in fitting the snaffle, fearlessly punch as many additional holes as necessary to reach the highest possible precision.

Curb Bits

THE STRAIGHT BIT should only be used if the chin groove canal is sufficiently comfortable for the tongue not to be crushed.
THE ARCHED BIT may be used with most horses.

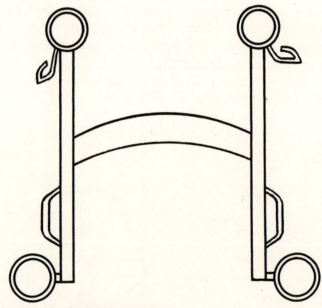

Curb bit with Arched Mouthpiece.

THE PORT-MOUTHED BIT is fine for bitting horses with a very thick tongue, narrow chin groove canal, or both.

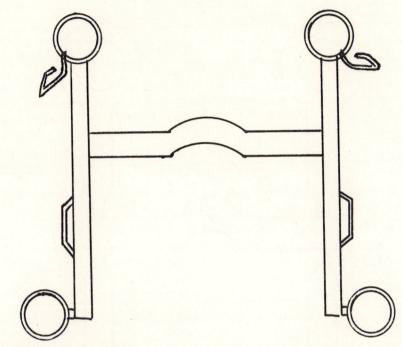

Port-Mouthed Curb Bit.

These three may have fixed mouthpieces in relation to their lateral cheeks, or mobile, then called SLIDING CHEEK CURB BITS and not very interesting in jumping. So let us forget about them and others with exceedingly long cheeks, there is enough power in upper cheeks measuring about 2 ins., the lower from 3 to 3¾, 4 ins. at most. Such dimensions, however, are valid only when the curb chain hooks are attached to the holes at the ends of the upper cheeks.

THE REVERSIBLE BIT merits special mention. More powerful than those above, it still belongs with the gentle bits, especially when not port-mouthed. Usable with or without bridoon, if employed for training and schooling it should be accompanied by a bridoon. Thanks to its elbowed cheeks, the lip strap becomes superfluous, and one of its benefits is that it rather prompts the horse to carry his head low, always a good thing in jumping where the rider holds his hands at withers level and the horse's mouth must be placed lower than the hands.

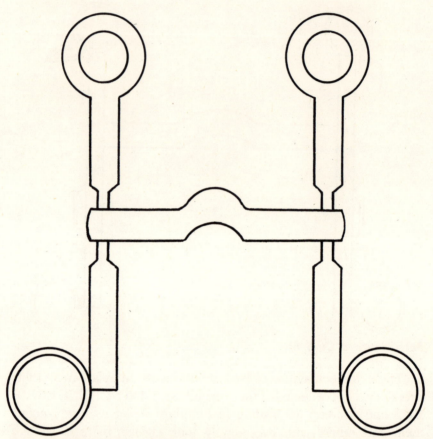

Port-Mouthed Sliding Cheek Curb Bit.

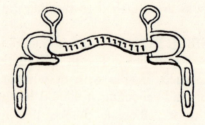

Reversible Bit.

Auxiliaries

The best known and most widely used are, of course, the *Standing*, *Running* and *Irish Martingales*, the *Running Reins* and *Gag Snaffle*. We describe them with the reservation that a well-trained horse does not need any of them and that they are useful only when one is forced to hasten training or to take a resourceful but difficult or incompletely trained animal over a horse show course.

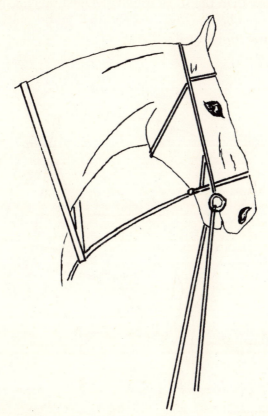

Standing Martingale.

They must be looked upon as temporary devices, not as the basis of a schooling method. Particularly harmful is the Standing Martingale which but confirms the horse more and more every day in his bad habit of raising his head, so that we shall not even discuss it.

THE RUNNING MARTINGALE may be used, yet only if cor-

rectly fitted. Too short, it acts when it shouldn't; too long, it fails
to act when it should. Short, to be exact, it has the same fault as the
Standing Martingale and prompts the horse to raise his head; long,
it serves no purpose at all. The fit is right when, the rider keeping
his hands in place, the reins tighten it without themselves being
incurved by it. Used this way it is but "an auxiliary component of
the snaffle whose power it increases without robbing it of gentleness: forming a channel which guides the horse." With new riders
or those with errant hands, it limits faults of hand, a very fine thing
in itself. Rather than the scorn usually heaped upon it, it should be
granted some publicity and be widely used by beginners, provided
they know how to adjust it.

Running Martingale.

THE IRISH MARTINGALE is made up of two rings large
enough for the snaffle reins to slide easily, connected by some flat
butt about 5 ins. long. Placed between mouth and neck, it is mostly
used on racehorses to keep them from raising their heads, then
abruptly lowering them and their necks, whirling all reins onto
one side. It only acts when necessary, so that the horse does not

fight against a solid point, though its passivity is perhaps its only drawback; for it keeps the reins from ending all up on one side, without, however, keeping the horse from plunging and turning with his head. When using it, or the Running Martingale, we need *leather rein stops* to keep the rings of these auxiliaries away from the mouth.

THE RUNNING REINS are chiefly a training gear, consisting of a pair of reins going from the rider's hands to the girth where they are attached, passing through the snaffle rings and between the forelegs. Their purpose is not just to keep the horse from raising his head, but to have him lower it to the point desired by the rider; that is, to obtain the *ramener*. Their rôle thus is "active," not passive, a very powerful instrument and therefore of delicate use and recommended only for very good riders. Its main drawback is the danger of overbending, of bending the poll at the wrong place, and—if the legs lack strength to maintain good impulsion at all times—the gradual result may be a ewe-neck, since the horse will continually tighten, rather than relax, the lower neck muscles. If used, an extra pair of ordinary reins must be put onto the snaffle rings by which we work the horse, the Running Reins acting solely when the horse attempts to change the right head position.

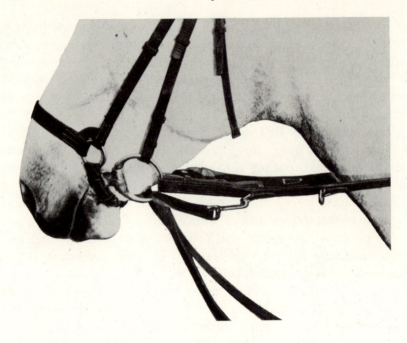

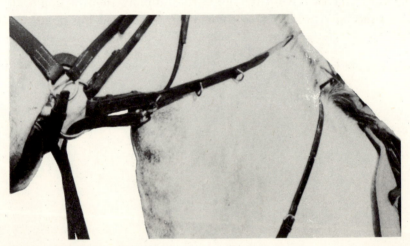

Market Harborough

THE MARKET HARBOROUGH is rather widely used, similar
to the Running Reins but less powerful, and thus less dangerous.
I feel, however, that its disadvantages are also almost the same
and that it does not really achieve any more than a correctly
fitted Running Martingale. The horse carries a *hunting breast-*

plate and a pair of reins (usually *German web reins*) attached to the snaffle rings. Each rein has three small rings spaced between mouth and withers. The auxiliary reins are attached to the ring of the breastplate (the one at breast level), then pass through the snaffle rings, then are each attached to one of the ordinary reins by small rings allowing for a more or less slack fit.

THE GAG. Here the cheek-pieces are not attached to the snaffle rings but pass through them and the reins are directly buckled to the ends of the cheek-pieces. When the rider tightens the reins, the snaffle bit rides up in the mouth. Its purpose is to dominate a puller or bolter and to combat the raising of the head. Since it makes

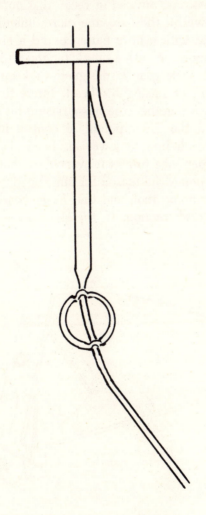

Gag Snaffle.

proper contact difficult, we often end up with a horse behind the bit, even if we put a second pair of buckled reins onto the snaffle rings.

THE HACKAMORE does not act on the mouth but on the lower face, an obvious help in skirting the difficulties of an extremely sensitive mouth. When combined with a snaffle, it reinforces its action.

By now we have already enumerated more bits and auxiliaries than we are likely ever to need and must remember that some of them are only meant for training and schooling, and there solely to reach a definite goal more quickly and safely. Some are of general use; but before choosing any, let us recall that none are miraculous, that the more powerful they are, the more difficult and dangerous their use, and that with a little patience and a great deal of work we can manage any horse with a simple bit and without special gear.

Practically all such gear is designed to keep the horse from going too fast and/or raising his head. Interestingly enough, the two evils usually go together, the horse raising his head, leaving his rider helpless and the bit impotent to control him. The remedy seems to be to teach him to lower his head. There is no doubt whatever, and experience proves it every day, that *the horse fights against any solid point,* the reason for our rejection of the Standing Martingale as a training tool, and that *he responds to any pull on his mouth by inverse traction.* If, therefore, backward and down-

Drop Noseband.

ward traction is exerted, he will react by a forward and upward traction. All such restraining instruments can give real service only to a very good horseman who has long known how to stop a horse with a simple bridle and how to make him lower his head. Improperly used, the cure is worse than the ill.

Some prefer a full bridle to a snaffle and there are differences of opinion on which model Pelham to choose and when; but, except for the Running Martingale with a simple snaffle, I do not see what the auxiliaries could give that good schooling could not, whose effects, at any rate, are less ephemeral. There are exceptions, but exceptions are the business of very experienced horsemen.

The Spurs

This is the time to introduce the spurs which the horse must learn to know and to respect. They are but the prolongation and reinforcement of the legs, though on occasion they may punish, their action ranging from a *prick* to an *attack*. They must never intervene merely by a lack of steadiness, unwittingly or against the rider's will, or remain glued to the horse's flanks. Beginners are not alone in misunderstanding their purpose, thinking of them as a necessity with a cold horse, an instrument in constant use. As with the curb bits, once the horse becomes enured to the gentle type, they pass on to more aggressive ones. They are as wrong as can be, for both spur and bit are to render the horse lighter to the hand and legs; and both, if improperly used, make him not only heavier to handle but very possibly restive. Legs and hand are expected to be tactful enough to shade their actions; this subtlety of intercourse between horse and rider is what curb bit and spur are supposed to serve, not to make possible a cruder language than with simple snaffle and spurless heel.

As in bits, there is great variety in spurs, from the gentlest (Prince of Wales) without rowels, via toothless rowels or with teeth of varying length and sharpness, all the way to those with rowels whose sharp teeth are long and few. As with the bits, it is usually the gentlest, not the severest, which give the best results. The length of the neck must be proportionate to that of the rider's leg—long leg, long neck—so that the spur can make contact without a great shift of leg. When using roweled spurs, make sure that dirt and hair do not clog and keep the rowel from turning freely, lest butchery ensue. I have seen many a rider on both sides of the ocean wear spurs without so much as knowing how to put them on, let alone how to use his legs, but greatly mystified at the poor results obtained. The spur rests of the boots are almost always too high; the branches of the properly adjusted spur are higher than the neck, the buckle on the outside of the foot, not on top or, heaven forbid, on the inside. The right kind of spur for the wearer placed in the right spot, if the heel is kept just slightly down and the toes not ridiculously outward, will not continually tickle or bother the horse. When one wants the neck to touch the flank he need but slightly turn the toes out, hardly raising the heel, yet still lower than the toes, to make the action of the spur felt. It is rarely necessary to go any farther. A warning has been conveyed, confirming an action of the leg to which the horse has not responded, telling him that if he does not respond now an attack will follow. With sensitive horses the contact of the inner branch suffices and one arrives this way at the point where the horse yields "to a faint whisper of the boot." Of the spur we might say as of the curb, that "it is a device allowing the rider to produce an effect of a given intensity through an effort of lesser intensity."

When first we introduce our pupil to it, we pick the gentlest and apply it after light leg action with moderation but neat clarity, small raps "elastic as those of the spring hammer of an electric bell." As soon as this contact is accepted without perturbation we can profitably give the *Lesson of the Spur*. A good lesson, well given, without brutality, yet with authority, should suffice, though we must not hesitate to repeat it in the course of schooling whenever the horse grows indifferent to the legs.

This lesson consists in a brief but energetic attack of *both spurs at once*. Reins in one hand to let us hold on to the pommel for stability, we use our legs in simple pressure of our calves, following this up immediately with an attack of the spurs. At the moment of contact with the flanks, we advance the hand holding the reins so the horse won't find a hindrance to his forward movement. Don't check him too soon, play dead on his back for about sixty yards, pat and check him progressively. Remain at a walk once or twice around and then, being likewise prepared, let your legs act but not, this time, the spurs. Usually he will "spurt" forward; pat him, return to the walk and then to the stables. If he does not react, use your spurs once more; but I really never had to attack twice in one lesson. The horse's present knowledge of the curb and spurs, his awareness of the former's power and fear of the latter's attack combined add up to what might be called, respect for the trainer's "weapons."

Boot with well-fitted spur.

CHAPTER TWENTY

Hands and Legs

Before we go on, let me make sure that we all agree on the definition for a "steady hand" and its important rôle in relation to the legs which are accorded such preponderance by most authors and instructors, for the good reason that such emphasis inculcates into the rider that without impulsion, without forward movement, equitation becomes impossible ("No impulsion, no horse!") and that it teaches him the use of his legs and rids him of the habit of moving his hands, hand movements coming so much more naturally than those of the legs whose use in everyday life, though important, is much less varied and skilled.

Take the soccer novice whose leg skill and precision are far inferior to those of his hands which, ever active, probably contract while he makes the effort of kicking the ball. But since his hands have no rôle in the exercise, their contraction does not impair his action and so his full attention may be allowed to focus on the education of his legs. The rider, however, holds the reins while using his legs, and at first he will invariably and by reflex use them to hold on and later—when a firmer seat lets him stay on without their help—still tend to move them while using his legs. Yet a mere stir, or even slight contraction of the fingers, is too much.

This is why written and oral instruction puts for a while a damper on the hands and stresses the action of the legs. But once the rider has acquired a good seat, his legs intervening by reflex, and the forward movement has become a fixed idea with him, equal importance must be assigned the hands whose skill decides the outcome.

The legs give the impulsion, but the hands store, channel, transform, and liberate it. However good the legs, if the hands are bad, so is the result; with a mouth stiffened by a faulty hand, the more the legs drive, the more they will stiffen the mouth. Their rôles thus complement each other, *and if there is no equitation at all without legs, there is no good equitation without good hands.*

This much about their importance. Now about their steadiness —in relation to the horse's mouth, not in relation to the rider's body or some part of the tack. They must be freed of all and any *useless* movement prompted by a jolt of the horse or just a contraction caused by the rider's unfortunate reflex. The expression, "the legs drive the horse onto the hand," means that the horse himself must tighten the reins through his rider's leg action and the hands should but receive this impulsion without ever drawing back. This, of course, is not enough, the receiving hand must also be pliant enough to make use of it. This really is the crux of the matter. The hand must not only be steady but *knowledgeable*, and the greater its sophistication the less the legs have to intervene, the difference between good riders much more in the science of their hands than in the energy of their legs. Licart writes in *Equitation Raisonnée*: "Not by driving obstinately against simultaneous resistances of both hands, literally fixed hands, and even less by pulling on a ewe-necked horse, do we get him to lower his head or make him hold back while further engaging his hind legs. Such procedures make it mechanically impossible for the horse to raise and lodge the base of his neck between the reins and thus to push at the loins and further engage the hind legs. The yielding of the hand, permitting the preliminary extension of the neck or the incurvations which disintegrate the resistance of certain neck muscles, bringing about the lowering of the head, quickly combat any such vices."

"Pull and kick!" as a summary of all equitation is a well-known quip among horsemen, inspired by what we just discussed. Of course, the comic effect of any caricature stems from emphasis on one feature and the ignoring, minimizing or deforming of the others.

CHAPTER TWENTY-ONE

New Rein Effects and the Raising of the Neck

Work and Lessons

THE WORK of the first year has consisted principally of rides; the walk, always extended, the predominant gait. Slow, cadenced, gradually longer trots, then canters strictly limited in duration and speed, leading up to twenty-minute canters at 350 yards per minute, without winding or wetting the horse. During these canters we have been looking for an extension of the strides, not a precipitation, by letting the neck go down more and more as the horse loosened up. By and by we have been climbing and descending more or less steep slopes at a walk during those excellent rides across country of all sorts, again letting at first an experienced horse precede us across dry and water ditches. Thus our horse enters his second year healthy and well-acquainted with all kinds of surrounding objects. He has not grown blasé, but fewer things startle him now and he is ever less liable to stop dead before a somewhat outlandish obstacle.

We now add faster canters twice a week. One mile, for instance, on each lead in quick succession, at 500 yards per minute. This, as everything else, of course requires a period of transition between régimes.

We now try him over the different natural obstacles we meet during rides, do our canters sometimes in a fence-dotted arena, which requires management and a preoccupation with the problems of balance and submission to the aids. Needless to say, the fences are not jumped but detoured.

THE LESSONS will now teach the horse to yield easily to the fourth and fifth rein effects, raise the base of the neck, enable him to perform the half-pass at the three gaits, to counter-canter and to do an isolated flying change of leg, all in the never-ending quest for more and more straightness.

The Fourth and Fifth Rein Effects

THE RIGHT COUNTER-REIN OF OPPOSITION, 4th EF-FECT PASSING IN FRONT OF THE WITHERS shifts the shoulders left, the horse's head being attracted to the right. In a reaction to the movement performed by the shoulders, the haunches are shifted right, unless the rider's right leg forms a wall opposing it, and the horse turns left by the sole shoulder movement. Done this way, the horse eventually turns on a penny, keeping his hind legs engaged.

THE RIGHT COUNTER-REIN OF OPPOSITION, 5th EF-FECT, OR INTERMEDIATE, PASSING BEHIND THE WITHERS shifts the shoulders and haunches left, without the horse changing direction. This is true if the wrist is positioned halfway between the places for a direct rein of opposition (acting on the haunches) and a counter-rein of opposition passing in front of the withers (acting on the shoulders). In this fifth effect, the more the direction of the active rein—the right in this instance—approaches that of a direct rein of opposition, the more it acts on the haunches and the less on the shoulders; the more it approaches the direction of the counter-rein of opposition passing in front of the withers, the more it acts on the shoulders, the less on the haunches. It is a most power-ful rein effect (provided the legs have brought the horse up to the bridle), giving us mastery over the horse, especially when he tries to gradually get out of hand or refuses to take the direction indi-cated. It also is the rein effect used for the Shoulder-In which forms the basis of the work on two tracks.

It is quite obvious, then, that third, fourth and fifth rein effects act either on the haunches, shoulders, or shoulders and haunches (that is, on part or all of the body), while the opening and neck reins act only on the head and neck and cannot be nearly as power-ful as the opposition reins which we therefore use in the second year for Schooling and performance. The opening and neck reins are used both in Training and on *haute-école* horses so highly schooled as to obey the slightest leg and hand action.

We now clearly see the importance of the "properly muscled" neck which bears comparison with a "tempered steel spring blade." Had we tried to supple the neck from the first lessons on, we should have ended up with a "rubber block" bending every which way at the slightest rein action, without the direction given it by our hands influencing the body in the least. Our opposition reins would today lose a great deal of their effectiveness and we would be spending our time trying to tauten this neck in hopes that then it would at least from time to time tighten the reins by itself. You must have ridden at least once a rubber-necked horse to understand the full importance of tautening the colt's neck before suppling it.

The Raising of the Base of the Neck

Extensions of the neck have been obtained by the chambon at liberty, and under the saddle combing the reins at the three gaits. These extensions are the foundation of the Schooling of the show horse who later will know how to bid for the reins in using his neck (as a tightrope walker would a balancing pole) before and during the jump. Moreover and above all, regardless of his specialty, a horse working with a low neck and giving neck extensions learns how to engage his hind legs under the mass. During these months of work (particularly when we have a colt or a young horse) the muscles of back, neck, and especially *the base* of the neck take on the proper orientation permitting later the raising of this base without the risk of "countersinking the withers" and of preventing the hind legs from engaging themselves because the back has meanwhile become hollowed out through a premature quest for this elevation.

For efficient, easy control of a horse, the base of the neck must obviously be placed between the reins, keeping the mouth below the hands, and therefore now, but only now, we endeavor to raise it. This need not be as pronounced for jumping as for *haute-école*. Actually, the jumper, needing his entire "balancing pole," should be *placed far and low*, the mouth slightly below withers level, since the rider's hands stay level with the crest and in front of the withers where they allow the neck the greatest liberty without the need to shift.

How do we obtain the raising of the neck? On foot and in the saddle.

ON FOOT, using a full bridle, we request at first an extension of the neck, easy to obtain when using the snaffle as follows: Standing at the horse's near side at head level, we slip the right snaffle rein over the poll, holding it with the right hand at about the level of the horse's left eye. The left hand holds the left snaffle rein just a little above the mouth. We close our hands over the reins and exert a slight continuous traction, our hands approaching each other, the left toward the ear, the right toward the mouth, acting through the reins on the mouth as would the chambon. As soon as the horse yields, our hands do likewise, accompanying the movement. The extension obtained, we let go of the snaffle reins and take only the curb reins, the right now toward the middle of the neck, the hands themselves acting toward this point or even in direction of the withers, no longer by continuous traction but by successive resistances, yielding slightly at the slightest raising, then resisting again till another raising is obtained, and so on. The idea is to obtain this raising progressively by alternate resisting and yielding of the hand.

UNDER THE SADDLE. When this exercise has been executed several times on foot, the horse having understood what his rider wants and yielded thereto, we repeat it in the saddle, preferably at first, as we did on foot, with the curb bit alone. The rider seeks the raising of the neck by raising his own hands and twisting his wrists upward till the fingernails are turned up. It is most important for the elbow to stay in place and the legs to drive the horse forward to engage the hind legs. This way we gradually get to where we have an elevation of the base of the neck, flexing at the poll and a correctly placed head with a face that side of the vertical, the whole permitting the bit to act with maximum effectiveness. We will have become, through alternate extensions and flexions of the neck, master of the "balancing pole," as we must be on the horse show course. If we want to keep a taut neck we must shun its lateral suppling. The neck, incurved from the base, *must remain taut*, and it will, if the outlined progression is followed, letting us obtain at will the engagement of the hind legs at half-halts while rounding a course and thus, by making us masters of the engagement of the hind legs, letting us remain masters of balance. We now have a submissive horse responding correctly to the action of our aids.

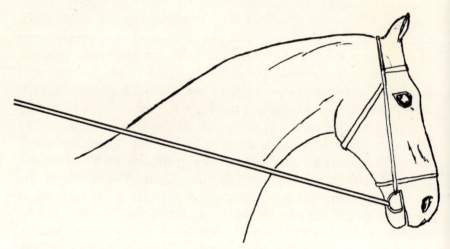

The placer **of the Jumper.**

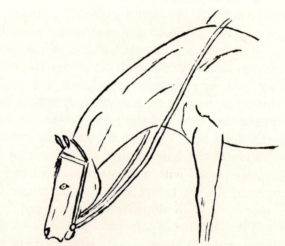

Extension of the Neck.

CHAPTER TWENTY-TWO

Suppling

All supplings are grouped in this one chapter, though some may have been started earlier, as, for example, the work on a circle done during the first year with a diameter suited to the horse's progress and disposition. The same is true for the relaxing at the jaw. The horse's training and schooling period is a unit that cannot be broken up into rigid compartments. We may, for example, on rides request occasional flexion of the jaw at a walk. By the time it comes easily at this gait we request it at a trot and canter.

Withal, the Schooling of a jumper requires less meticulous attention to suppling exercises than that of a dressage horse. Our aim is sufficient suppleness to yield easily to guiding signals and, above all, *to engage the hind legs on demand.* This suppling we divide into three principal categories:

1. Longitudinal suppling
2. Lateral suppling
3. Complete suppling.

The mobility of the haunches is sought and improved by the action of the single leg to which the horse must yield easily. (See p. 103)

We use the circle where the horse is led gradually to engage his inside hind. Working the stiffer side longer than the other, we begin on rather large circles. The outer leg bars the outward deviation of the haunches, the inner leg, around which the horse is bent, maintains the forward movement. Speed-ups and slow-downs on straight lines and circles are excellent.

F

We work a great deal at a trot, practicing the transition from trot to walk and vice versa, speed-ups and slow-downs at a trot, passing from trot to halt and from halt to trot without going through the walk, till eventually we can halt directly from the walk, trot and canter and strike off into all three gaits directly from the halt.

Rein Back

This is one movement we do not demand before we are well into the second year *and are sure that the horse keeps good contact on the bit*, and then first on foot, later in the saddle. Well done, it is an excellent exercise; but we must never forget that the first thing the horse must be taught is *not* to back. Once we start, we shall be content with a few steps, three or four at most. If the horse has so far been well-trained he should by himself return to the forward movement as soon as the aids cease to demand the rein back.

ON FOOT, standing in front of and facing the horse, we take the reins near the snaffle rings. We make him step forward two or three steps and through successive and alternate hand oppositions ask for one step back, without holding the head too high, leaving him all possible latitude for placing it. All we want for the moment is for him to understand our demand, permitting him to carry it out as easily as possible. During all this preparatory work, we make sure we ask for the rein back as follows: three steps forward, one step back, three steps forward. It must be ground into our pupil from the start that the smallest backward step is immediately followed by the forward movement. In sum, *the horse must be taught physically to rein back with an intense urge to step forward*.

IN THE SADDLE, we give maximum relief to the back by leaning more on the stirrups. Alternate hand action slows the walk to the utmost; then we request the rein back by this action. Most resistances are prompted by overburdening the quarters. The aim is to make the horse rein back straight, each diagonal commanded by a hand action on the rein corresponding to the acting diagonal, the horse stepping forward once more as soon as hand action ceases. The exercise gains its full value through the transitions from walk to rein back and from rein back to walk.

Suppling of the Forehand

THE MOBILITY OF THE SHOULDERS is obtained by changes of direction by neck rein, legs at their normal place, acting with strictly equal intensity, in order to maintain the forward movement. The haunches will thus always be affected by the change of direction, the horse turning at both ends. As he yields more and more easily to the neck rein and the single leg, we begin to keep the haunches from being shifted on the turns by using the single leg as a wall.

We will repeat this exercise on broken lines whose angles and lengths may be modified at will. When our horse has acquired a certain dexterity, we will ask him for progressively tighter half voltes, holding the haunches, to where they become, eventually, half-turns on the haunches. Thus we become able to swing the forehand from rein to rein as we shall do the hindquarters from heel to heel.

THE RELAXING AT THE JAW. There are two possible reasons for a contracted jaw: a muscular contraction elsewhere in the body which is reflected in the jaw, or a contraction originating in the jaw itself.

When relaxing at the jaw, the mouth opens slightly, allowing the tongue to lift, taking the bits along which click when they fall back into place. The tongue acts as in deglutition. This relaxing is to be obtained gradually by a tactful rider encouraging their slightest manifestations by a descent of the hand. We will work toward it at slow gaits, mainly on the circle, also on straight lines. Proving a complete absence of contraction, the relaxing at the jaw is the external sign of lightness.

We might find WEIGHT RESISTANCES caused by bad balance and to be counteracted by the use of half-halts; or FORCE RESISTANCES occasioned by muscular contractions to be remedied by vibrations on the snaffle bit. These vibrations are made, without the wrists, by a rapid, supple yet limited to-and-fro movement, fingernails down.

The horse can be taught and exercised in this relaxing at the jaw, while on foot. Difficult to do well, however, requiring great tact, it can do more harm than good and we shall not try them until we are sure we can prevent the slightest backward movement and obtain free forward movement at the slightest prompting.

The first exercise consists of getting our horse to slightly open his mouth by activating the tongue through inverse traction on the curb reins. We are standing to the left of his head, holding the left curb rein in our left hand, the right in our right. We exert with the right hand slow and continuous traction toward his neck, while the left exerts strictly equal traction in the opposite direction.

The second exercise: We put the buckle or seam of the snaffle rein on the horse's poll, right behind the headstall. Then we pass the reins through the rings of the snaffle bit and exert an almost vertically upward traction and wait for the tongue to activate.

In both exercises we yield as soon as the horse yields and are content with the merest indication of obedience. If our horse should begin to back, we desist immediately and make him advance, starting over a little further on. We must be careful that our tractions affect only the mouth, not the neck, let alone the entire body.

The *third exercise* is undoubtedly less academic, but also less dangerous. We put a full bridle with very short branches on our pupil before meals, and as he eats he will have to relax his jaw to perfection, without any danger of a backward flow of energies. Since he won't chew as well, of course, we should feed him his oats crushed.

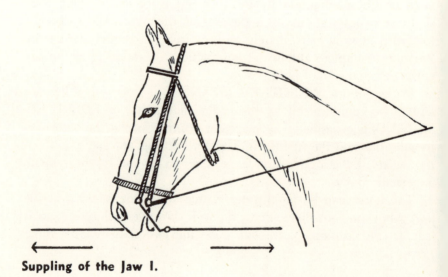

Suppling of the Jaw I.

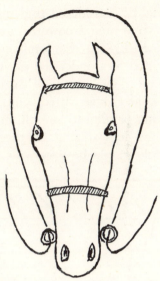

Suppling of the Jaw II.

The Work on Two Tracks

This work, known to all horsemen, which complements the suppling movements, is so important that we shall deal with it in some detail. Misunderstood or badly done, it not only is of no avail but better left alone.

In this work the forelegs are traveling on a distinct, parallel track from that of the hind legs. It pursues three aims:

1. To make the horse more adroit and consequently better balanced, teaching him to move sideways and to change sides easily.

2. To supple him generally.

3. To obtain the engagement of the hind legs.

It complements the work on straight and curved lines because it brings into *prominent* play certain muscles which are only secondary in one-track figures. Here we shall study only the *Shoulder-In* and the *Half-Pass*.

Depending on the inflection given to the horse in side-stepping and the direction followed, the different legs are called upon, one by one, to furnish the principal effort. Two-track work is futile before our horse is sure of his work on the circle which has promoted the engagement of the inside hind.

THE SHOULDER-IN

The Shoulder-In, rightly considered the complete suppling *par excellence* and at the same time a powerful means of domination, will untie the shoulders, lighten the forehand, supple back and loins and engage the hind legs under the mass.

The horse is bent all along his spinal cord and travels in the direction of his convex side. Once "fitted" onto his circle, and thus bent, he leaves it moving parallel to himself, maintaining the same inflection, fore and hind legs staying on their respective tracks. To begin with, the circle should be very wide.

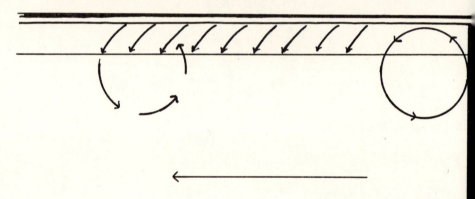

Shoulder-In.

THE LEFT SHOULDER-IN. We set the horse onto a left circle corresponding in size to the degree of inflection intended in the Shoulder-In. Just as the hind legs come into tangency with the track we request a few steps of the Shoulder-In, then desist and finish the started circle. The aids are:

The Left Rein (fifth effect) acts on the entire body which bends.

The Right Rein limits the inflection of the neck and, also the guiding rein, maintains the forehand on the track.

The Left Leg, around which the horse is bent, acts close to the girth, from back to front.

The Right Leg keeps the off hind from deviating.

The Body Weight is well-distributed, slightly accentuated to the right.

For a Shoulder-In, when not begun by a circle, we are careful to keep the inclination proportionate to the direction followed, about thirty degrees.

We constantly watch the inside hind which has the hardest task, that of staying the mass under which it must engage itself by a bending of the haunches, and which will try to evade the effort by skidding to the inside.

THE HALF-PASS

In the Half-Pass the horse is kept straight from head to tail, his head placed slightly in the direction of the shift, his position slightly oblique in relation to the traveling direction, his shoulders preceding the haunches. Such is the classical Half-Pass. In training, however, as a suppling aid, it may be performed with a slight bend to the side of the shift.

THE HALF-PASS TO THE RIGHT. The aids are:

The Right Rein, a slight opening effect, places the head and is the guiding rein.

The Left Rein, a neck rein, pushes the shoulders to the right (the direction of the Half-Pass).

The Left Leg, the determining aid, pushes the haunches to the right (the direction of the Half-Pass).

The Right Leg maintains impulsion, keeps the off hind engaged and from escaping to the right.

The Body Weight is accentuated on the right.

In the Half-Pass to the right the limbs of the off lateral are drawn together, those of the near drawn apart. The near hind has to make a greater effort than in the left Shoulder-In to cross its congener, especially if the latter is kept engaged by the rider's right leg. On the other hand, the near fore will cross the off more easily than in the left Shoulder-In.

As in the Shoulder-In, it thus is the leg which is crossed that regulates the work of the crossing leg. We therefore must be able to prevent any lateral escape and to determine with precision the advance of the leg to be crossed. Otherwise the two-track work loses almost all its value, does nothing but give the horse a certain agility in moving sideways, and this at the risk of blemishes where, through wrong placing, the limbs injure each other.

HEAD TO THE WALL. Here the forelegs stay on the track while the hind legs are traveling on an inner track. The oblique described must at first be of about thirty degrees, gradually reaching forty-five. It would be wrong to require too much of an angle to begin with, as it would impair the forward movement which must always remain intact in the work on two tracks. Keep this in mind as you work.

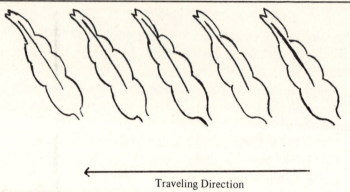

Traveling Direction

Head to the Wall.

We slow down, the *right leg* setting the quarters on the inner track.

The Left Rein, an opening rein, obtains the placing and is the guiding rein.

The Right Rein, a neck rein, pushes the forehand to the left and limits the placing given by the left.

The Left Leg, close to the girth, ensures continued impulsion.
The Right Leg pushes the haunches in the direction of the Half-Pass.

The Body Weight is accentuated on the left.

We end the Half-Pass with the *left leg* which places the haunches back behind the shoulders.

We take advantage of the corners to position our horse for the Head to the Wall, rather than by right leg action which would cause the quarters to swing around the forehand.

TAIL TO THE WALL. Now without a wall for guidance, things become a little more difficult. Here too the angle must be slight to begin with, not ever reaching more than forty-five degrees. The forelegs are now on the inner track. The results of this exercise are a measure of the horse's obedience to reins and legs.

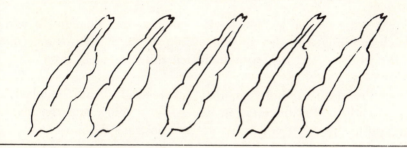

Traveling Direction

Tail to the Wall.

ON THE DIAGONAL. The forelegs are traveling on the diagonal and the hind legs on a parallel track, the horse's body remaining parallel to the long sides of the ring. In the beginning the haunches may lag a little, to make sure they will not precede the shoulders, of which there was little danger in Head and Tail to the Wall. We must, however, achieve complete straightness if ever we should want to go on to the Counter-Change of Hand on two tracks.

We do not start into the Half-Pass on the Diagonal until the whole horse is parallel to the long walls, then give him the correct placing for the Half-Pass and shift the shoulders before shifting the haunches. The time lapse between both requests must, however, be minimal. In rejoining the opposite track (which the forelegs must reach at least twenty feet before the corner) we do not stop leg action until the hind legs are once more behind the shoulders. This way the horse is perfectly straight before taking the corner, while otherwise he could not be adjusted to the curve.

Accustoming the horse to obeying with alacrity to the aids but never to anticipate a movement, we interrupt the Half-Pass here and there on the diagonal and request a few straight forward steps, then half-pass once more in the same direction. Or during a Half-Pass to the left, we request a few straight forward steps, setting the horse perfectly straight while they last, parallel to the long walls, then reverse the aids and request a Half-Pass to the right.

THREE RULES. Impulsion should always be total in all work on two tracks. To reestablish it, do not hesitate to cut off in mid-movement.

Do not look for too much of a bend in the Shoulder-In and watch carefully over the correct position of the outside lateral (off in the left Shoulder-In), without which this movement loses much of its value.

In the classical Half-Pass, the horse's head should be placed just slightly in the direction in which he is going, and the hand prompting this must not by its action constrain the movement of the outside shoulder or counteract the shift of the haunches.

THE DISTRIBUTION OF THE WEIGHT. Depending on the inflection given the horse for the direction followed, the distribution of the weight on the legs changes. Moving to the left in a right Shoulder-In, he bends to the right, the off hind determines the movement to the left, but it is overburdened (concave side). The same hind determines the movement to the left in the Half-Pass to the left, but here it is on the convex side and lightened to the same degree. Taking this example, the near shoulder is lightened in the Shoulder-In and overburdened in the Half-Pass.

The Work at the Canter

The main goal of the lessons at a canter is to make our horse equally comfortable on both leads. The introduction to the canter will come that much more easily; and once he strikes off as well on one lead as the other, we may broach single flying changes of leg. This is as far as we shall go in the intended training.

The main difficulty of the canter stems partly from the horse's natural inflection, compounded by the "drift" occasioned by the gait.

Not seeking rectitude as perfect as in academic horsemanship, we may use either the diagonal or the lateral inside aids in striking off into the canter, the former being easy and not requiring as advanced training as the latter.

We have trained our young horse to strike off on the near lead, using, for example, right leg and rein (lateral outside aids). Though traversing the horse a bit, these aids were more easily understood. By and by we have stopped use of the right rein and begun to use the left instead, thus keeping the neck straight and in the direction to follow. The right leg no longer shifts the haunches to the left, as it used to, but only keeps them from being thrown to the right, serving at the same time as a signal for the departure at the canter on the near lead. The demand is now up to the left (inner) leg which acts at the girth. This way our horse is able to strike off into the canter on a given lead, remaining straight.

Once this has been achieved on the track, we must achieve it far from the wall and while hacking. A good way to judge our pupil's balance and submission is to request the departure at the canter now on the near, now on the off lead, not like clockwork— which would become routine and lose all value—but in irregular sequence. We must be able to check to the trot after barely three or four strides of the canter and to pass into the canter after a few beats of the trot. Once he performs this easily, he is ready for the counter canter and single flying changes.

THE COUNTER CANTER is an excellent suppling exercise, furnishing absolute proof of the horse's stability at the canter. It makes him change his balance by himself and affords the alternation of release and engagement that interests us. We prepare for it by cantering on broken lines, gradually emphasizing the turns taken at the counter canter inherent in this figure. Then comes the serpentine. Difficulties are usually encountered only if the rider starts this work before the horse is perfectly settled in his canter or if he has been allowed to change lead, improperly at times, at the slightest change of direction.

When it comes to hand action, it must be borne in mind that for the counter canter the horse needs more freedom than for the canter proper. The whole exercise must be devoid of constraint which would warp and render it useless. If the horse changes lead, check to the walk and start all over at the same spot. Return to less sharp curves, if necessary; but no punishment and no impatience. Here more than elsewhere we need calm; by the time we introduce him seriously to the flying changes, he would remember any adverse reaction. Since we wish through gymnastics to enable him to turn easily in good balance at the counter canter, we should on no account seek the solution in constraint. Maintaining a slow progression we shall obtain a complete serpentine on the center line, the half volte, and the half volte in reverse, without a change of leg. When we finally get to the volte, the jumper's training on the flat is nearing completion.

CHAPTER TWENTY-THREE

Single Flying Changes of Leg

The jumper does not absolutely need the flying changes, as long as he is able to turn at the counter canter. Since, however, they can only do good, no harm, I do think it a fine idea to teach him to give them correctly.

By the time he is so perfectly exercised in the counter canter as to experience no difficulty in changing the lead on which to strike off at short intervals, teaching him the single flying change becomes so easy that it does not constitute a waste of time in schooling.

I know that changing lead on the course is time-consuming; but if the horse disunites himself in taking a turn at the counter canter, the balance is jeopardized. Besides, without consulting us, he will anyhow have taken the time for a change of limb, usually the fore. So isn't it preferable to teach correct changes we may prompt if and when necessary?

In order to obtain, not wrest, a flying change of leg from the horse, we should

— on A LEFT CIRCLE with a radius of about 15 ft. request a strike-off on the OFF LEAD (thus the counter lead);

—cadence the canter with the RIGHT REIN (the rein which places the horse in this case);

— leave the LEFT LEG PASSIVE;

— CHANGE the placing of the horse's head and USE THE LEFT LEG (as for the strike-off on the near lead);

— leave the RIGHT HAND AND LEG PASSIVE;

— leave the SEAT PASSIVE.

The horse will give us a perhaps somewhat fumbling change from outside to inside leg, but he will have understood. We pat him profusely and then start over, on the same circle, on the same hand. The ease of his flying changes will be commensurate with the quality of his balance and on the introduction to the strike-off he has received. Therefore, if the flying changes come too hard, we must go back to working on the strike-offs.

If all goes well, we proceed to changing, on the contrary, from the inside (correct) to the outside (counter) lead.

On a left-hand track we request the change on the straight line and continue on the counter lead through and beyond the corner. Little by little we request the change closer and closer to the corner, till he performs it inside the corner. We then take up this exercise on the circle, first a wide one, alternating requests and hands; that is, the near should be now the inside, now the outside lead.

This winds up the jumper's work on the flat which, summed up in a single sentence, has rendered submissive to the aids a horse sufficiently suppled to obtain the engagement of the hind legs and to manage it with ease. Any movement not involved in this endeavor is not only superfluous but often harmful in the lessons.

SCHOOLING OVER THE FENCES

CHAPTER TWENTY-FOUR

The Work at Liberty and Under the Saddle

The first year's training over the fences had but one purpose, to give the horse good form. The second year's schooling aims should lead to the utilization of his physical aptitudes developed by the work and improved by the form he has acquired at a trot over the fences.

The gait for these lessons will from now on be the canter, three lessons under the saddle to each lesson at liberty. At first the height is that of the last lessons at a trot (about 3 ft. and a width of 3½ ft.). The number of weekly lessons is still two, going up to three at year's end, but the number of obstacles jumped at each lesson still does not exceed ten, if we want to neither blemish nor dishearten our horse. Since the progression must be based on possibilities and age and our example is that of a young horse, these ten obstacles are an absolute maximum. When we work an older horse (who has already shown) in the dead of winter, to prepare him for the following season, we may take up to thirty fences in a week, though in *three* lessons of *ten*.

The height of the fences should throughout the year remain well below that of the first shows, a level which, in slow progression, should be reached only *toward the end*. While nothing could be worse than jumping too high, one or two fences should be cleared at every day's lesson before returning to the stables. The twice-weekly obstacle lessons are preferably given after the work, so the horse is well limbered up; but the work should be carefully dosed, on those days, to limber up without overtaxing him. The return to the stables invariably follows these lessons, making him appreciate the rest and reward and associate them with the effort furnished.

The Work at Liberty

This is given in the ring and, if possible, in a (usually oval) jumping lane. At all events, we must manage to have a few fixed obstacles for schooling. I know of, and sympathize with, the widespread aversion against them. The military, working with a quantity of horses belonging to the state, could afford to ruin a few; the civilian owner of two or three valuable mounts cannot. But there are two kinds of fixed obstacles; some are merciless, but some, while punishing a fault, do not inflict real damage. Their construction makes the difference. After all, the cross-country fences of the Three Day Event are fixed and competing horses are schooled over fixed fences; all is in not disheartening the horse nor making him jump beyond his capacities. Generally (not always) when the horse is not taken beyond his powers he has greater respect for the more massive of two non-fixed obstacles, though they be of equal height. Over natural obstacles, ditches with or without water, capped by fixed bars or without, as long as they remain within his possibilities, he rarely commits a fault, at least at liberty.

The purpose of our kind of schooling over fixed fences is to make him respect a straight fence of light poles no less than a *Trakehner Graben*. For two years I made eight horses I had under training jump fixed obstacles once a week and never had an accident. The best way is to mix fixed and non-fixed fences, changing their locations and interchanging their respective places, not ever letting the horse know beforehand which will fall and which will not. Even in the lane, where one might be tempted to set up only fixed fences, it is better to use both sorts; a horse who has tumbled two or three times over a straight jump with deceptively harmless poles will become wary and approach all fences with more caution. The horse commits his greatest faults during the rising phase, knocking into the bar above the knees, invariably knocking down the pole. There are two ways of teaching him to place the summit of his trajectory slightly in advance of that of the obstacle. We may place a guard-rail at the foot of the obstacle or an iron rod level with the upper bar of the straight fence but slightly in front of it. The first manner is not recommended because it teaches the horse to reckon with the foot of the fence, not, as he should, its summit. The second is fine if the thin, hollow iron rod is placed about ten inches ahead of the upper bar, and the whole is set up so the wooden pole is clearly visible and the iron rod blends into the general silhouette of the obstacle. It is a sort of static rapping and should be done as follows: Place between two ordinary jump standards two wooden poles four inches in diameter. Lest the iron rod stand out too clearly, everything is painted black and white. We place the iron rod in front, held up by two additional standards, slightly lower than the wooden pole so that approaching the obstacle it cannot be seen, blending into the lower part of the wooden pole behind. Quite obviously, though the knee-caps should be kept,

Fence with Iron Rod.

the boots should be taken off, if we want the horse to react the next time. This way we are teaching him to reckon with the summit of the obstacle and even somewhat in advance of it, which gives us a certain safety margin in negotiating straight fences.

WATER JUMPS AND BROOKS are first negotiated with the

longe, easier on horse and rider. My advice, if not that of all horse-men, is to let the horse wade in the puddles found outside and eventually to make him put all four feet into the exercise water jump, then cross it at a walk. As obstacles go, the water jump is usually easy; its difficulty lies in what it is made of; i.e., water. We must rid the horse of his fear of it; then we place at the foot, on the take-off side, a small brush, putting the horse on the longe, into the canter and, in a little foot race, make him jump it three or four times. After a few such sessions we may take off the brush, put on bars or not, sure he will jump it fearlessly. Familiarity with the element is the main thing; for there is really little danger of his stopping in mid-course to indulge in wading.

THE BANKS are approached with equal precautions. The longe is not too helpful here, unless our training bank is rather small and we can go up with the horse and jump first while an assistant drives him on to follow. If not done just right, quite comical situations ensue, and at any rate we rarely have a bank of the right dimensions.

One of the simplest and most effective methods is to post two assistants with training whips on top of the bank, then to canter off behind an experienced jumper firmly but not too fast over three

The bank at Hickstead.

or four fences and when he is nicely in the forward movement to
follow the other up the bank. The ascent, when not too steep, does
not usually pose problems. These begin on top from where he is to
jump down. If he stops despite the example of his comrade, the
assistant makes him jump, without turning this help into punishment or terrorization which, obviously, would be the worst lesson
the horse could receive. Three or four times of this should do away
with the problem of taking the bank, whether upward or downward.
Three-fourths of all difficulties spring from poor training. If the
horse responds keenly to the legs, has never run out or, trying, was
stopped short and made to feel the spurs, why would he suddenly
make trouble? As in everything else, we follow, of course, a slow
progression and our first banks will hardly look like that at Hickstead.

The Work Under the Saddle

Initially we jump at the canter single obstacles of unchanged
height. We let the horse manage by himself, merely keeping the
reins taut and maintaining direction, impulsion and speed, now at
450 yards per minute. When such single, but extremely varied,
fences are cleared easily, then and only then may we take on small
rounds of six or eight, also doubles, later trebles without tricky
distances, increasing height and difficulty gradually till we get to
the level of the first public shows.

During these exercises on such small, familiar obstacles with
a horse now calm and in confidence we first teach him to take off
from close or standing off (short or long strike-off), extending or
shortening the strides, always prudent, never asking for too much
in one lesson. He is already accustomed to extending and shortening his strides on the flat, and now that he understands what is
expected of him and yields without constraint, this exercise is
repeated over the fences. If tact was needed in the early stage, it
now must be all-pervasive; and tact is what is hardest to explain.
I can describe a given movement, for example, and if you are already endowed with some tact, you will perform it better than
another not so gifted but who, understanding, still can perform it
somehow, if not very well. But to explain tact itself, the reflexes,
and what one ought to feel, is impossible because intangibility is
the very nature of reflex and feeling. Now, usefully regulating

strides and placing the strike-off are principally matters of feeling one's horse, being able to establish with him a constant conversation. Tactless, we may try to get by with the outer signs of such a conversation, but those sham gestures are not likely to give valid results.

CHAPTER TWENTY-FIVE

Reward and Punishment

I have often spoken of the need for calm without impatience, for frequent rewards at one and any show of obedience. I have particularly emphasized reward, because all books on equitation, mine included, say a great deal about punishment. Sometimes they say too much, and too little of reward, so essential in training, particularly in the early period and with a colt. Every time I mention calm and confidence I am addressing riders who bully their horses because they confuse disorder with energy. Energy, though of the essence, must manifest itself in calm. The horse must like his trainer, trust and respect him without fear or apprehension. Certain moral properties must combine with technical if a horseman would be called a skillful trainer. Sooner or later there comes the day in any training when the horse rebels against the master's demands. These revolts may spring from completely divergent, but few, sources. Our example being a truly green young horse, we are not retraining an intractable, badly trained animal whose bad habits are the harder to combat as they have taken root a long time ago. Such horses require trainers sufficiently experienced with their kind to use strong medicine without killing the patient. Our colt, however, is not in need of ferocity. One point is important and worthy of our constant surveillance: that part of training which takes place in the stables and at first is really more important than that in the ring. Later, and throughout all of Training and Schooling, they still are of equal importance. Often difficulties in the ring originate in the stables; but if nothing is wrong in those quarters they may originate in

a) some physical discomfort or defective sight;
b) an excessive demand on our part;
c) a playful character;
d) a weakness on our part;
e) his difficult character.

As with all ills, before we try to find a remedy we must determine the origin. The veterinarian can enlighten us quickly and well concerning physical discomfort and eye defects.

If we have overtaxed our horse's faculties we simply must backtrack to the point before trouble set in and take a few days before we take any forward steps, in cautious installments, content with the slightest progress. If, rather than try to be as stubborn as our horse, confounding pigheadedness with perseverance, we know how to backtrack in time, no great harm is done.

There are playful horses. We should beware of them. At first they are cute; later they become terrors. The basic thing is not to play with them, no more than with the others, by the way. Horses aren't playthings. If they take the initiative and we are not permissive in the beginning, the habit is soon broken. In this respect, too, we should watch the stables where grooms sometimes love to play with and tease the horses.

If the trouble stems from having yielded to a defense, we must urgently reimpose our will.

Intractable horses are few, but they exist, and we either entrust their training to a more competent man, or are determined to emerge as victors from this struggle, whatever the cost. Which are the defenses a horse can employ against his trainer? The most dangerous is rearing, embellished at times with a whirlabout; restiveness which opposes the force of inertia to the rider's leg action, making it impossible for him to prompt the forward movement; kicking up; bucking. The run-away is a horse of a different color, a vice not to be classified under the heading of defenses proper. Obviously, the remedy to all defenses is the forward movement which disintegrates the worst and mitigates the rest. But for the forward movement to be fully valid it must be obtained instantly and irresistibly. Some powerful means must affect not only the horse's physique but also his spirit, the horse under domination realizing his own impotence. This result can be attained by several means.

THE RIGID REINS are the simplest and most effective. Even a mediocre rider can use them successfully. They are fashioned from two smooth wooden sticks, about one inch in diameter, long enough for one of the ends, when the other is tied with a little strap of butt to the holes at the ends of the upper branches of the bit where the curb chain hooks are attached, to be held in our hand, without having to hunch when the horse's head is stretched rather forward. When we want to drive him forward we use our legs and simultaneously push our hands forward more or less energetically, depending on the degree of the defense. The horse, drawn forward, will yield to their irresistible action and the quarters will simply follow the forehand. This is the moment to associate leg and spur action with that of the rigid reins. After a few days, they may be dropped because then the legs alone suffice to prompt the forward movement. They also serve to make the horse turn when he refuses to do so by simply pushing the left rein forward to turn right, while drawing the other as much toward oneself. Since the purpose of these reins is to stretch head and neck forward, the forehand is overburdened and makes rearing impossible. They are of simple use, their result is immediate and they afford domination of the horse's most dangerous and hardest to defeat defenses. If there exists many a means to slow down a horse, there are but few to drive him forward. The rigid reins are anything but new, they were invented before the turn of the century; and whereas there are other means of subduing a strong head, they require a vigorous and experienced horseman.

Anyway, for the preservation of the horse it is always preferable to avoid such stormy sessions. The ultimate purpose of all training is to teach the horse to yield to the rider's will and thus the crux of the matter is to impose ourselves upon him. Since the cardinal point is moral domination, we must act according to his character and early reactions. Depending on our knowledge and tact, we obtain more or less complicated movements more or less easily, sooner or later and, eventually, more or less perfectly. But whether elementary or highly sophisticated training is intended, the combined will of horse and rider must originate with the rider, not the horse. Reaching this mastery takes rather more gentleness and patience with some horses, a few come to it quite naturally, others only after a struggle which should be as brief as decisive. No sooner the horse enters into revolt, he must become aware of his impotence.

I fondly remember a small stallion, built like an athlete, whom I used for a long time as a school horse. For several months he had been carrying pupils on his back in the riding hall when, one day, on a hack he took it into his head to stop and back, without the slightest attention to his rider's desperate efforts. I stopped my little troop, entrusted my own mount to the hapless horseman and mounted. A rough talking to with whip, spurs and voice, all at once, obtained the forward movement. My pupil remounted and I kept him by my side for the rest of the hack with never a squeak out of his valiant steed. Later I lost sight of this little stallion till I happened to hear that he was for sale, having become impossible, biting and kicking everything and everyone within reach. I went down, bought and rode him back to my own place. At the first sketchy defense I closed my legs and called his name, and he did not budge again. He had recognized me. As of the following morning I put him into my classes and never, whoever rode him, did he try to bite or kick while I was where he saw or heard me. This is just one example among many, one of the most typical. The rider, more so the trainer, must know how to impose himself or training becomes impossible.

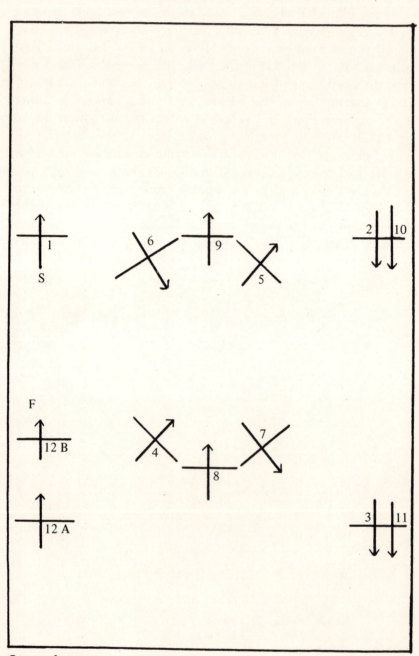

Course Layout

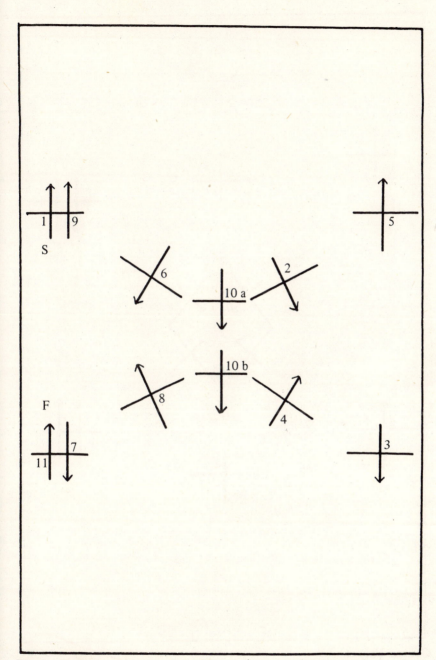

Course Layout

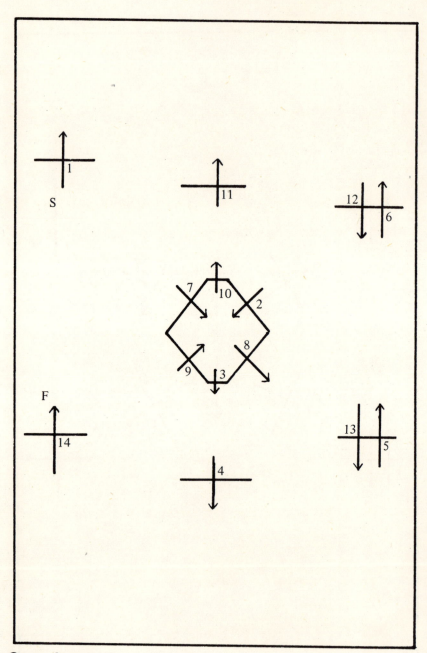

Course Layout

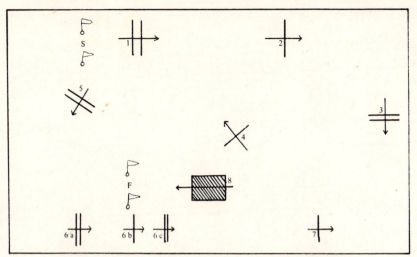

Course Layout at World Championship in Buenos Aires.

1. **Brush spread**   1 m 20 x 1 m 30 x 1 m 80

2. **"Toronto" fence**   1 m 50

3. **Rustic oxer**   1 m 40 x 1 m 50 x 2 m

4. **Post and rails**   1 m 50

5. **Wall (with poles)**   1 m 40 x 1 m 50 x 2 m

6a **Spread**   1 m 40 x 1 m 70

6b **Post and rails**   1 m 50

6c **Oxer**   1 m 40 x 1 m 50 x 1 m 70

7. **Post and rails**   1 m 50

8. **Water jump**   4 m 50

Distance between 6a and 6b: 10 m 60
Distance between 6b and 6c: 7 m 20
Length of the course: 390 meters
Time allowed: 67 seconds

NOTE: I am giving all the measurements in meters because the metric system is officially used by the F.E.I. For my American readers, here is a table of approximate equivalents:

1 m 20	4′	1 m 72.5	5′ 9″
1 m 27.5	4′ 3″	1 m 80	6′
1 m 35	4′ 6″	1 m 87.5	6′ 3″
1 m 42.5	4′ 9″	1 m 95	6′ 6″
1 m 50	5′	2 m 02.5	6′ 9″
1 m 57.5	5′ 3″	2 m 10	7′
1 m 65	5′ 6″	2 m 17.5	7′ 3″

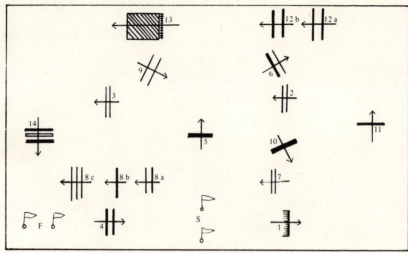

Course Layout at Tokyo Olympics, 1964.

1.	Brush jump (with pole)	1 m 30
2.	Birch oxer	1 m 35 x 1 m 40 x 1 m 50
3.	Upright wattle	1 m 50
4.	Oxer of barriers, with red and white poles, over a water jump	1 m 40 x 1 m 40 x 1 m 70
5.	Blue and white checkered panel	1 m 60
6.	Birch oxer	1 m 45 x 1 m 50 x 1 m 45
7.	Red wall	1 m 60
8a	Oxer of green and white poles with a take-off (grey wall and wattle)	1 m 40 x 1 m 45 x 1 m 35
8b	Wall	1 m 50
8c	Triple bar	1 m 50 x 1 m 70
9.	Oxer of barriers	1 m 50 x 1 m 50 x 1 m 70
10.	Gate (with poles)	1 m 50
11.	Grey wall	1 m 50
12a	Green and white oxer, with take-off pole	1 m 40 x 1 m 45 x 1 m 45
12b	Oxer	1 m 50 x 1 m 50 x 1 m 50
13.	Water jump	5 m
14.	Oxer of red and white poles over a beige wall	1 m 45 x 1 m 45 x 1 m 85

Distance between 8a and 8b: 7 m
Distance between 8b and 8c: 10 m
Distance between 12a and 12b: 7 m 50
Length of course: 870 meters
Time allowed: 1 minute 57 seconds

If the Buenos Aires course seems easier, do not forget that the World Championship finalists had to complete this one three times with completely strange horses.

Part III

The World of Jumping

Capt. Cariou (France) on Mignon, first Gold Medalist, Show Jumping, 1912. (Photo Sport Universel)

William Steinkraus on Sinjon, individual gold medal in Mexico. (Photo L' Année Hippique)

Frank Chapot on San Lucas. (Photo Irish Times)

David Barker on Franco. (Photo Irish Times)

G

Marion Mould (the former Marion Coakes) on the pony Stroller, individual Silver Medal in Mexico. (Courtesy Leslie Lane)

**David Broome on Mister Softee, individual Bronze Medal in Mexico.
(Courtesy Leslie Lane)**

Major de la Doucette on Gare-a-Lui, Cadre Noir. (Courtesy Col. de Saint André)

**Jonquères d'Oriola on Ali-Baba, Gold Medals Helsinki and Tokyo.
(Courtesy French National Studs)**

Graziano Mancinelli on Water Surfer.
(Courtesy Federazione Italiana Sport Equestri)

Raimondo d'Inzeo on Merano, Aachen 1964.
(Courtesy Mr. Raimondo d'Inzeo)

Piero D'Inzeo on Fidux.
(Courtesy Federazione Italiana Sport Equestri)

Figueroa Castillejo on Itapiro.
(Courtesy Spanish Federation of Equestrian Sports)

Amorós on Zeiss.
(Courtesy Spanish Federation of Equestrian Sports)

Goyoaga on Kif-Kif, First World Champion, 1953.
(Courtesy Spanish Federation of Equestrian Sports)

Winkler on Torphy. (Photo Mitschke)

Schockemöhle on Zukunft, wall at 2 m 10. (Photo Mitschke)

Steenken on Simona.   (Photo Leslie Lane)

Here are the results of the major traditional jumping competitions and records since 1912. I would like to thank *L'Année Hippique* for supplying me with much of the information and the American Olympic Committee for allowing me to do research in their archives. I also used Dr. Ferenc Mezö's excellent book *"The Modern Olympic Games"* and Mr. François-Achille Roch's very well-documented article in *L'Information Hippique*. In spite of all this valuable assistance I have not managed to find the names of the winning horses in the 1912 and 1920 Olympic Games. Because of an old rule the military rankings of medalists are not given in the official results. In order to avoid mistakes I have had to follow this practice for the earliest games.

Actually, the rules governing Olympic competitions have varied over the years and the reader will sometimes be surprised at the tabulations. In 1920, for example, Lt. Lequio was first in the individual competition—but he was not on the Italian team. This is because at the time there were separate events for the individual and team championships, and the competitors were not always the same.

Also, the excellence of my sources notwithstanding, names are often misspelled. I corrected mistakes to the best of my knowledge, but there are probably some left. For this I am sorry.

There are, as you see, imperfections in this compilation. I thought, however, that many riders would like to have a general picture of the Olympic Games since their renewal.

To complete this, I am giving the results of the world championships, of much more recent foundation (1953). They are preceded by a short explanation of their nature.

Finally, I have listed the world records for the high and broad jump.

The Olympic Games

The modern games were begun by Baron Pierre de Coubertin, who in 1889 had been asked by his government to study "universal physical culture." The first games took place in Athens in 1896—that is, 1503 years after the last ones of antiquity. The ensuing Olympics were in Paris (1900), St. Louis (1904) and London (1908), but it was not until 1912 that equestrian games in the modern sense appeared. The credit for their inclusion goes to Count

Clarence von Rosen, who was later to become Honorary President of the F.E.I.

Listed first are the individual medalists, then the teams. The rider's name is followed by that of his country, and then his horse's.

THE OLYMPIC GAMES

STOCKHOLM—1912

1—Mr. J. Cariou	France	Mignon
2—Mr. von Kröcher	Germany	Dohna
3—Mr. E. de Blommaert de Soye	Belgium	

1—SWEDEN

Mr. C. Lewenhaupt	Meduse?
Mr. H. von Rosen	Lord Iron
Mr. G. Kilman	Gatan
Mr. F. Rosencrantz	Draba

2—FRANCE   Mignon
Mr. J. Cariou
Mr. d' Astafort
Mr. Meyer
Mr. Seigner

3—GERMANY
Mr. S. Freyer
Mr. von Hohenau
Mr. Deloch
Prince Friedrich Karl von Preussen

ANTWERP—1920

1—Mr. T. Lequio	Italy	Trebecco
2—Mr. A. Valerio	Italy	Cento
3—Mr. G. Lewenhaupt	Sweden	Mon Coeur

1—SWEDEN
Mr. H. von Rosen
Mr. C. König
Mr. D. Norling

2—BELGIUM
Mr. de Oultremont
Mr. Commans
Mr. de Gaiffier

3—ITALY

Mr. E. Caffaratti	Traditore
Mr. G. Cacciandra	Fortunello
Mr. A. Alvisi	Raggio di Sole

PARIS—1924

1—Mr. A. Gemuseus	Switzerland	Lucette
2—Mr. T. Lequio	Italy	Trebecco
3—Mr. A. Krolikiewicz	Poland	Picador

1—SWEDEN

Mr. A. Thelning	Loke
Mr. A Stähle	Cecil
Mr. A. Lundström	Anvers

Paris continued

2—SWITZERLAND
Mr. A. Gemuseus — Lucette
Mr. W. Stüber — Girandole
Mr. H. Bühler — Sailor Boy

3—PORTUGAL
Mr. B. d' Almeida — Reginald
Mr. M. de Souza — Avro
Mr. M. d'Albuquerque — Hebraico

AMSTERDAM—1928
1—Mr. F. Ventura — Czechoslovakia — Eliot
2—Mr. P. Bertran de Balanda — France — Papillon XIV
3—Mr. Ch. Kuhn — Switzerland — Pepita

1—SPAIN
Cap. de los Trujillos — Zalamero
Cap. J. Morenes Navarro — Zapatoso
Mr. F. García — Revistado

2—POLAND
Lt. Col. C. Gzowski — Mylord
Mr. K. Szoszland — Alli
Mr. M. Antoniewicz — Readglet

3—SWEDEN
Lt. K. Hansen — Gerold
Mr. Björnsterna — Kornett
Mr. E. Hallberg — Loke

LOS ANGELES—1932
1—Mr. T. Nishi — Japan — Uranus
2—Mr. H.D. Chamberlin — United States — Show Girl
3—Mr. C. von Rosen, Jr. — Sweden — Empire

(No team medals were distributed: not a single national team had three riders who could complete the course, and they were all eliminated.)

BERLIN—1936
1—Lt. K. Hasse — Germany — Tora
2—Lt. H. Rang — Rumania — Delphis
3—Cap. J. von Platthy — Hungary — Sellö

1—GERMANY
Lt. K. Hasse — Tora
Mr. M. von Barnekow — Nordland
Mr. H. Brandt — Alchimist

2—NETHERLANDS
Mr. J. de Bruisse — Trixie
Mr. H. van Schaik — Santa Bell
Mr. J. Greter — Ernica

3—PORTUGAL
Mr. L. Mena e Silva — Fossette II
Marquis de Funchal — Merle Blanc
Mr. J. Beltrao — Biscuit

LONDON—1948

1—Col. H. Mariles Cortes	Mexico	Arete
2—Cap. R. Uriza	Mexico	Hatvey
3—Chevalier J. d'Orgeix	France	Sucre de Pomme

1—MEXICO

Col. H. Mariles Cortes	Arete
Cap. R. Uriza	Hatvey
Mr. A. Valdes	Chihuchuc

2—SPAIN

Col. García Cruz	Bizarro
Col. Navarro Morenes	Quorum
Maj. Ponce de León	Foratido

3—GREAT BRITAIN

Col. H. Llewellyn	Foxhunter
Lt. Col. H. Nicoll	Kilgeddin
Maj. A. Carr	Monty

HELSINKI—1952

1—Mr. P. Jonquères d'Oriola	France	Ali-Baba
2—Mr. O. Cristi	Chile	Bambi
3—Mr. F. Thiedemann	Germany	Meteor

1—GREAT BRITAIN

Col. H. Llewellyn	Foxhunter
Mr. W. White	Nizefela
Mr. D. Stewart	Aherlow

2—CHILE

Mr. O. Cristi	Bambi
Mr. R. Echeverreira	Lindo Peal
Mr. C. Mendoza	Pillan

3—UNITED STATES

Mr. J. Russel	Democrat
Mr. W. Steinkraus	Hollandia
Mr. A. McCashin	Miss Budweiser

STOCKHOLM—1956

1—Mr. H.-G. Winkler	Germany	Halla
2—Lt. R. d'Inzeo	Italy	Merano
3—Cap. P. d'Inzeo	Italy	Uruguay

1—GERMANY

Mr. H.-G. Winkler	Halla
Mr. F. Thiedemann	Meteor
Mr. A. Lütke-Westhues	Ala

2—ITALY

Lt. R. d'Inzeo	Merano
Cap. P. d'Inzeo	Uruguay
Cap. S. Oppes	Pagoro

3—GREAT BRITAIN

Mr. W. White	Nizefela
Miss Pat Smythe	Flanagan
Mr. P. Robeson	Scorchin

ROME—1960

1—Cap. R. d'Inzeo	Italy	Posillipo
2—Cap. P. d'Inzeo	Italy	The Rock
3—Mr. D. Broome	Great Britain	Sunsalve

1—GERMANY
Mr. H.-G. Winkler	Halla
Mr. A. Schockemöhle	Ferdl
Mr. F. Thiedemann	Meteor

2—UNITED STATES
Mr. G. Morris	Sinjon
Mr. F. Chapot	Trail Guide
Mr. W. Steinkraus	Ksar d'Esprit

3—ITALY
Cap. R. d'Inzeo	Posillipo
Cap. P. d'Inzeo	The Rock
Cap. A. Oppes	The Scholar

TOKYO—1964

1—Mr. P. Jonquères d'Oriola	France	Lutteur B
2—Mr. H. Schridde	Germany	Dozent
3—Mr. P. Robeson	Great Britain	Firecrest

1—GERMANY
Mr. H. Schridde	Dozent
Mr. K. Jarasinski	Torro
Mr. H.-G. Winkler	Fidelitas

2—FRANCE
Mr. P. Jonquères d'Oriola	Lutteur B
Miss J. Lefebvre	Kénavo D
Cap. G. Lefrant	Monsieur de Littry

3—ITALY
Maj. P. d'Inzeo	Sunbeam
Cap. R. d'Inzeo	Posillipo
Mr. G. Mancinelli	Rockette

MEXICO—1968

1—Mr. William Steinkraus	U.S.A.	Snowbound
2—Miss Marion Coakes	Great Britain	Stroller
3—Mr. David Broome	Great Britain	Mister Softee

1—CANADA
Mr. Day	Canadian Club
Mr. Gayford	Big Dee
Mr. Elder	The Immigrant

2—FRANCE
Miss Lefebvre	Rocket
Mr. Jonquères d'Oriola	Nagir
Mr. Rozier	Quo Vadis

3—WEST GERMANY
Mr. Winkler	Enigk
Mr. Schridde	Dozent
Mr. Schockemöhle	Donald Rex

The World Championships

The championship is decided after four events, three of which are preliminary and select the four finalists. The first three tests are like ordinary show jumping events: often they consist of one "cup" course, a handiness test judged by table B or C, and a Grand Prix type course. In the finals the four riders have to do the course four times, first with their own horse, and then with each of the other finalists' horses. The faults of all four rounds are added up, and the rider with the smallest total is declared World Champion.

Thus the champion will not only be able to ride well his own mount, but must also possess the tact to get the most out of three completely unknown horses. These three strangers have often been ridden and trained in a manner completely foreign to him. He is allowed to ride them for only three minutes (and jump two fences) before entering the ring. He may use his own saddle, but the bitting of the horse must remain the same.

This different kind of event was first used during the *"Fête Mondiale du Cheval"* in Paris in 1953. While it has stirred up some controversy, most riders and trainers support it as the best way to select a true champion.

The "championship" formula was invented by Chevalier d'Orgeix who, with several other riders, tried it out on the *L'Etrier* grounds, in Paris after World War II. The "jury" was General Donnio. The "finalists" were, besides d'Orgeix, the Count de Maillé, Major Saint-Fort Paillard and Georges Calmon. De Maillé, who won, called this kind of event a "technical match."

WORLD CHAMPIONSHIPS

PARIS—1953

1—Mr. Francisco Goyoaga	Spain	Quorum
2—Mr. Fritz Thiedemann	Germany	Diamant
3—Mr. P. Jonquères d'Oriola	France	Ali-Baba
4—Cap. Piero d'Inzeo	Italy	Uruguay

MADRID—1954

1—Mr. Hans–Guenther Winkler	Germany	Halla
2—Mr. P. Jonquères d'Oriola	France	Arlequin D
3—Mr. Francisco Goyoaga	Spain	Baden
4—Cap. S. Oppes	Italy	Pagoro

AACHEN—1955

1—Mr. Hans–Guenther Winkler	Germany	Orient
2—Lt. Raimondo d'Inzeo	Italy	Merano
3—Maj. Dallas	Great Britain	Bones
4—Mr. P. Jonquères d'Oriola	France	Voulette

AACHEN—1956

1—Cap. Raimondo d'Inzeo	Italy	Merano
2—Mr. Francisco Goyoaga	Spain	Fahnenkönig
3—Mr. Fritz Thiedemann	Germany	Meteor
4—Maj. Carlos Delia	Argentina	Discutido

VENICE—1960

1—Cap. Raimondo d'Inzeo	Italy	Gowran Girl
2—Lt. Col. Carlos Delia	Argentina	Huipil
3—Mr. David Broome	Great Britain	Sunsalve
4—Mr. William C. Steinkraus	United States	Ksar d'Esprit

BUENOS AIRES—1966

1—Mr. P. Jonquères d'Oriola	France	Pomone B
2—Mr. Alvarez de Bohorques	Spain	Quizás
3—Maj. Piero d'Inzeo	Italy	Bowjak
4—Mr. Nelson Pessoa	Brazil	Huipil

The World Records

The F.E.I. was founded in Paris in November 1921. The first records it witnessed were those of Lt. de Castries, in the high jump and the broad jump. It did, however, recognize at least the main ones established before its time.

The potential record-breaker is allowed three tries at the fence in his official attempt. For the high jump, the obstacle is vertical to 1 meter 30. Then the poles rise at an angle of 33 degrees, triple-bar style. The broad jump layout is the following: the water is 6 meters, and the brush preceding it is widened to make the greater breadth.

The year is followed by the place where the record was established. Then come the rider, his nationality, and his horse. The measurements are given in meters, because that is how they were officially recorded.

WORLD RECORDS

High Jump

1906 PARIS	Cap. Crousse (France)	Conspirateur	2 m 35
1912 VITTEL	Mr. F. de Juge—Montespieu (F)	Biskra	2 m 36
	Mr. R. Richard (France)	Montjoie III	2 m 36
1933 PARIS	Lt. Ch. de Castries (France)	Vol-au-Vent	2 m 38
1938 ROME	Cap. A. Gutiérrez (Italy)	Osoppo	2 m 44
1949 VIÑA DEL MAR	Cap. A. Larraguibel (Chile)	Huaso	2 m 47

Broad Jump

1912	LE TOUQUET	Mr. H. de Royer (France)	Pick Me Up	7 m 50
1935	SPA	Lt. Ch. de Castries (France)	Tenace	7 m 60
1946	BUENOS AIRES	Mr. Fraga Partrao (Argentina)	Guaraná	7 m 70
1948	BILBAO	Maj. Nogueras Márquez (Spain)	Balcamo	7 m 80
		Cap. F. Muestre Salinas (Sp.)	Faun	7 m 80
		Maj. Nogueras Márquez (Spain)	Balcamo	8 m 00
1949	THE HAGUE	Mr. B. van der Woort, jr. (N)	Coeur Joli	8 m 10
1950	BILBAO	Lt. Col. Nogueras Márquez (Sp.)	Balcamo	8 m 20
1951	BARCELONA	Maj. F. López del Hierro (Sp.)	Amado Mío	8 m 30

Glossary of Technical Terms

The following are definitions of terms constantly repeated in this book. Extension by long usage has slightly deformed the sense of some, though their general meaning has been preserved. Others —describing related but totally different situations—are too often used interchangeably and have become a constant source of error and misunderstanding. Some date back centuries, but even the more recent ones derive in content from the works of the great masters of the eighteenth and nineteenth centuries.

BALANCE   This definition has been given in length on page 20.

BEAT   The noise each foot makes when touching down.

COLLECTION   A state in which engagement of the hind legs and *ramener* coincide. This definition makes it obvious that true collection cannot be achieved after six or eight months' hasty work aimed at giving the head and neck a flattering attitude, without attention to the hind legs which come bumbling and dragging after, a kind of equitation liable to fool the layman, not the horseman.

ENGAGEMENT   This definition has been given in length on page 20.

IMPULSION   This definition has been given in length on page 19.

COORDINATION   The correct use the rider makes of his legs, hands,
OF THE AIDS   and body weight, so combining them that each complements and reinforces the two others in obtaining precise execution of a given movement.

LIGHTNESS   The horse's perfect obedience to the slightest indication of his rider's hand and heels. This term, thus, applies to the rider's use of his aids to which the horse yields completely and with alacrity, not, as is often believed, to the lightness of contact with the bit, a confusion of lightness and light contact. It is particularly dangerous since some make scant use of their legs so that they may keep their reins hardly taut and obtain a sensation of "lightness," while they actually have a floating horse without impulsion. In reality, lightness of contact is but one of the consequences of genuine "lightness."

PLIANCY   Also called, *Correspondence,* the result of the rider's seat and steadiness (or fixity) which permits him to "go with the horse" in all circumstances.

RAMENER   An attitude taken by the head at the rider's demand and made possible by an inflection at the poll (occipital-atlas and atlas-axis joints). The face must approach the vertical, never go beyond it. It must be caused by the advance of the body toward the head, never vice versa. An otherwise good English word for this, *Head Carriage,* has the drawback of frequent confusion with *Self-Carriage,* the natural way the horse carries his head.

SEAT   The horseman's basic quality which permits him to stay on his mount whatever its reactions. The essential characteristic of the seat should be suppleness. Mark here the difference between seat and correspondence (pliancy); i.e., the difference between staying "on one's horse" and "with one's horse."

STEADINESS   The absence of any needless or involuntary movement. Not to be confused with immobility which signifies absence of all movement. The somewhat more technical term for this, *Fixity,* is, alas, liable to contribute to this confusion in the amateur mind.

STRIDE   "The space covered in a complete step, constituting its length, measured from one toe to the other of two successive imprints of one and the same foot." (Jacoulet & Chomel.) The stride of the canter, constituting a full step, consequently, is of three times plus a period of suspension.

TAUT HORSE   A combination of psychological and physical factors springing from *channeled impulsion.* In this state, the back transmits the impulsive forces of the quarters integrally to the forehand, where the reins gather them up. Without losing suppleness of neck, the horse maintains a free and trusting contact with the bit.

Bibliography

Traité d'Hippologie, Jacoulet et Chomel, Gendron & Cie. Saumur.
Questions Equestres, Gen. L'Hotte, Plon-Nourrit & Cie., Paris.
Obstacle, Conduite et Style, Chef d'Escadrons Gudin de Vallerin, Henri Neveu, Paris.
Clear Round, Dorian Williams, Hodder & Stoughton Ltd., London.

Index